The Legacy of John Holt

Contributors

Thomas Armstrong

Peter Bergson

Alexander W. Clowes, M.D.

Aaron Falbel

Patrick Farenga

Theo and Anita Giesy

Peggy Hughes

Susan and Larry Kaseman

Merloyd Lawrence

Roland Meighan

Jerry Mintz

Berrien Moore III

Kirsten Olson

Wendy Priesnitz

Susannah Sheffer

Kirk Talbott

Nelson "Bud" Talbott

Strobe Talbott

Vita Wallace

Jenny Wright

The Legacy of John Holt

A Man Who Genuinely Understood, Trusted, and Respected Children

Introduction by Kirsten Olson

Edited by Patrick Farenga and Carlo Ricci

Copyright © 2013 by Patrick Farenga and Carlo Ricci All rights reserved

Cover photo by Maggie Sadoway taken at a Holt Associates open house on Feb. 9, 1984. The children from left to right: Joshua Gray, Solon Sadoway, Chris Gray, Danette Finn, an unidentified child, and Bridget Finn.

Published by HoltGWS LLC, Medford, MA

ISBN-13: 978-1-7321885-1-8

Printed in the United States of America

HoltGWS
Medford, MA 02155
www.johnholtgws.com

Dedication

For Day, Lauren, Alison, and Audrey, whose love and understanding help me with everything I do.—Patrick Farenga

To Gina, Annabel, and Karina. For making a great life a wonderful one.—Carlo Ricci

Contents

Foreword xi

Introduction xv
    Kirsten Olson

Learner-Managed Learning 1
    Roland Meighan

Music Comes Naturally and Technique Can Come Later 15
    Vita Wallace

King of the Renegade Philosophers 23
    Interview with Bud, Strobe, and Kirk Talbott, and Alec Clowes

We Drag Mathematics About until Everyone Is Put to Sleep ... 35
    Interview with Berrien Moore

Cracker-Barrel Writing 41
    Thomas Armstrong

Learner-Centered Schools 47
    Jerry Mintz

A Close Family Friend 49
    Peggy Hughes

What Else Do You See? 55
    Merloyd Lawrence

The Nickel and Dime Theory about Social Change 59
    Wendy Priesnitz

Photographs 65

John Holt and The Politics of Homeschooling 71
    Susan and Larry Kaseman

Going to Court and Changing the Law for Homeschooling ... 79
    Theo Giesy

John Holt Saved My Life 91
    Peter A. Bergson

A Friend Who Nurtured Learning 99
    Patrick Farenga

What I'm Left With 107
   Susannah Sheffer

A Man Who Saw Things Clearly 115
   Aaron Falbel

Homeschooling Makes It Easier for Your Life to Be All of a Piece 125
   Jenny Wright

Foreword

We, Pat Farenga and Carlo Ricci, decided to coedit this book as a celebration of John Holt's life and work. We believe that whether you were lucky enough to know John personally or whether you only know John through his work, this book offers many insights and will serve to inspire, as John clearly continues to do. Equally, if you have never heard of John, or are just beginning to be introduced to him, this book will set you on a new path.

Carlo Ricci teaches graduate students at the Schulich School of Education, Nipissing University, and he tells his students that if they never read anything again, they should at least read something by John Holt. As a result, many do read him, either formally in a course or on their own, and the impact is almost always stunning. John's writing is clear, accessible, and powerful. He was able to use language to explain and slice right through difficult ideas and thoughts as easily as a hot knife melts through butter.

His ideas are not only clear but, for many of us, they awaken what has been lying dormant within us for so long. In Ricci's case, John's works acted as a gentle yet powerful ally to help support what Ricci was feeling. John provided Ricci with the courage to feel and think the thoughts he was having, and to be proud and confident that what he was feeling needed to be expressed out loud. There is no doubt that John's relevance and his oeuvre continues to inspire his readers. He makes the complicated and murky, less so.

As an example of this continued inspiration, we, along with Stephen Tedesco, are working on making all 143 issues of *Growing Without Schooling* (GWS) magazine available in volumes as print books and e-books. John founded *GWS* in 1977 and it was the first magazine published about homeschooling and learning outside of school. As we were working through this, it became clear to us very quickly that this is not something that we can complete without plenty of help. When we put out a call for volunteers we were hoping to get 30 or 40 people interested and we thought that we would start slowly until eventually we would reach the goal of converting all 143 issues. We are now at over 100 volunteers and counting and, despite the tremendous amount of time and tedious work required, people are telling us that because "it's John" they want to help. Many have shared how John and his writing have been and continue to be an important part of their lives and so they would like to give back. To us, this speaks to the tremendous influence and respect John Holt deservedly commands.

We want to sincerely thank all of the contributors to this volume for agreeing to share with us their personal experiences with John Holt. It became clear very quickly that John touched many of the lives he came into close contact with in very deep ways. Without their powerful stories and willingness to share, this book could not have been written. We thank them for sharing their stories and for helping us either remember or know for the first time what a brilliant mind and delightful friend John was to so many. We also would like to thank them for being open in sharing his humanness that some may, in some cases, find quirky while others find inspirational. For those of us encouraged by John's work, we are grateful to the contributors for these insights within their pieces.

For Pat Farenga, who was fortunate enough to spend so much time with John and who still deeply feels his loss, this book has allowed him to revisit the life of a close friend. For Carlo Ricci, who never met John but wishes more than anything that he had, it has also allowed him to gain insights into the life of a wonderful human being. As for Pat and Carlo, working together on projects with the hope of sharing John and his works with the world has resulted in a friendship that we both value and that might not have happened had it not been for John. Just like he brought us together, he continues to bring people together in formal and informal ways, as large and as small groups, and for this we are thankful. We are thrilled to have played a part in bringing this fond and caring group of people together in this book for you, in the hopes that those who understand how important it is to trust children, and those who know John and his work, will continue to come together in increasing numbers until we are heard, and the result will inevitably be a better world for all.

Patrick Farenga published *Growing Without Schooling* magazine and numerous other publications related to homeschooling, unschooling, and learning outside of school from Holt's death in 1985 until 2001. He continues to keep Holt's ideas alive by writing, speaking, and publishing through HoltGWS LLC and www.JohnHoltGWS.com.

Carlo Ricci is a professor of education and currently teaches in the Graduate Program at the Schulich School of Education, Nipissing University. He edits and founded the *Journal of Unschooling and Alternative Learning*. He has written and edited a number of books including *The Willed Curriculum, Unschooling, and Self-*

Direction: *What Do Love, Trust, Respect, Care, and Compassion Have To Do With Learning*; and *Turning Points: 35 Visionaries in Education Tell Their Own Stories* (AERO, 2010) with Jerry Mintz. He has also written numerous articles on unschooling and self-directed learning. He lives in Toronto, Ontario with his wife and two children.

Introduction
By Kirsten Olson

To those who have been lucky enough to discover John Holt, many view him as one of the great philosophers of the American educational establishment. Although insufficiently read in teacher preparation programs, he is often wrongly regarded as a radical or boutique philosopher. In my experience, he is understudied in educational philosophy courses, and currently unknown to the vast majority of nearly three million teachers in the United States. I truly believe that Holt is among the great philosophers of education of the 20th century: moving beyond Dewey and more accessible (and deliberately so); like Montessori in some respects, although without her understructure of actual schools, because Holt explicitly moved away from a belief in conventional schooling and the establishment of schools per se. An inspired observer of teaching and learning—a truth teller and a truth-seeker—Holt's popularity was and remains with the "people" and among a certain group of educational iconoclasts: parents of children in school who question its paradigms, critical-thinking students who chafe at school's strictures and intellectual diminishments, and adults who seek to understand the effect of the institution on them and society. In spite of Holt's determined marginalization by many in the academy, Holt's works have cumulatively sold over a million-and-a-half copies since the mid-1960s, some have never gone out of print, and a few have been translated into 14 languages. What accounts for the schism in readership and awareness of John? What made Holt such a memorable, deeply influential and in many cases, life-shaping influence on so many educational reformers, as the essays here testify? What were the qualities of his writing and thinking that influenced the course of education in the 1960s and 1970s, and may have something to say to us now? And where do you fit in? This volume, for you, may be an act of discovery.

As this group of essays indicates, Holt was many things to many people: a defender of the inherent rights, dignity, and brilliance of children; a fearsomely energetic camping buddy who enjoyed hurtling through the woods at a brisk pace and bringing down a bird with a rock (can such exploits really be true except in fairy tales?); a political and philosophic pole-star to many educational iconoclasts of the late 1960s and 1970s. This collection offers many pleasures, some of them images of John Holt taking a sponge bath in his apartment on Chestnut Street, and then pouring the grey water onto his compost on his terrace for his worms; of John comfortably stopping by Peggy Hughes' house on Sparks Street for a cup of afternoon tea after teaching at Shady Hill; of an enthusiastic musician and playmate to child musician Vita Wallace, as they banged out tunes on a green upright kitchen piano and enjoyed knock-knock riffs on a violin as part of the Bedchamber Players. Playful, observant, fierce, tender, free-thinking—in this volume Holt begins to emerge as a real person whom the reader might imagine meeting, conversing with, going to visit in his apartment on Chestnut Street and, ultimately, coming to appreciate as a pragmatic philosopher of learning, a generous and far-seeing mentor, a political strategist, and a passionately keen observer of the human mind in the act of learning.

John Holt was among the great observers of the enterprise of teaching and learning. His brilliance of observation, his eloquence, his simple belief in the human mind, and his fascination with the journey of learning made Holt, in his time, profoundly popular and influential. Within the pantheon of important radical education writers of the 1960s and early 1970s, John Holt and Ivan Illich were perhaps the most significant, because of the clarity, boldness, and profundity of their vision of a more ideal human culture, a self-sustaining, courageous, convivial human society more explicitly in balance with the larger physical and spiritual ecosystem.

Things we are now "discovering" about teaching, and optimal cognitive environments for learning, were in many cases foreseen and predicted by this group of writers, and by John Holt in particular. Serious readers of Holt, for instance, will note that his views on the importance of pleasure in relation to learning, his ideas about how teaching can interfere with learning (in Holt's view, teaching was very strong medicine that could quickly become poison); and the psychosocial means through which teacher beliefs about pupils predict and create performance, are truths about human cognition now being proven in learning labs around the world. The work of Sugata Mitra, Mihaly Csikszentmihalyi, Martin Seligman, Daniel Goleman, Claude Steele, CASEL, Yong Zhao, Barbara Fredrickson, and Brene Brown, point to social neurobiological constructs that John Holt and many of his colleagues "knew" before there were fMRIs, clinical trials, and peer-reviewed journal articles to prove them. The burgeoning field of social neuroscience increasingly tells us that how we feel about learning, our teachers, the power relations in the learning community, and the environment in which education is constructed matter tremendously to what is learned and understood. In the conventional classroom, many of these elements are counterproductive to us, even if they are swiftly normalized by us as learners. That we as students and teachers find this slippery, and quickly become acclimated to counter-productivity and dysfunction—we often don't even notice that we are growing stupid in school—Holt understood and described in ways that are unforgettable to many of his readers.

Holt's experiments with his own neuroplasticity—believing he could learn to play the cello at age of 40, when conventional wisdom said this was not possible, have now been corroborated by many studies on the plasticity of the brain throughout the lifespan. Holt's appetite for experimentation, his defiant belief in what was possible, and his capacity for truthful and grounded observation of the learning process explored in his many books and other writings helped him "know" and stretch what was possible. The revolution in our understanding of cognition that we are witnessing in education—with the necessary rethinking of the conventional classroom, the questioning of the idea of teaching itself, and in the presumptions that underlie most conventional teaching (that students "need" something from adults, their teachers) were prefigured by the radical education writers of the 1960s. And as a writer and observer, John Holt was perhaps the greatest among them—the most eloquent, wisely simple, and free-seeing. Holt is waiting to be discovered again by generations of students, families and educational communities impatient with the physical and psychic boundaries to learning still erected by school.

HOLT THE MAN

Holt's relatively straightforward life, described by various essayists here, belies the complexity and impact of his thinking. Born of upper middle class, East coast parents, he attended a privileged private boarding school and an Ivy League university (Holt wished not to reveal the names of these schools); served in WWII, became a political activist after the war and then—as so many do—fell into teaching and (somewhat unexpectedly) into writing a book about his observations on teaching. None of these details indicate the breadth of his intellectual life, his plainspoken and planted-in-compost radicalism, his outreach as he wrote thousands of letters to an immense audience of interested parties and acolytes over nearly four decades—nor his impact on a time in American history when many ideas about how to live were up for grabs. (My own grandfather, approximately Holt's age, also religiously composted in New York City, took a broad and unusual range of vitamins and supplements daily, had a horror of any kind of preservatives in food, and considered the car an unnecessary and wasteful modern convenience.) Holt was a part of an era of American life when many individuals were recalibrating their relationships to the major institutions and memes of modern commercial life.

THE ESSAYS

Here, in a set of 16 essays that celebrate Holt's impact 29 years after his death, we glimpse various versions of John, and various meanings individuals attached to him, his ideas about education, and most especially their constructions of the meaning and purpose of life after interacting with him. These pieces, from homeschoolers and academics, people who worked at Holt Associates in Boston, to those who met him during his travels around the world in the 1960s through the early 1980s, represent a beginning, an attempt to chart the meaning and impact of Holt as an influential writer and philosopher, a visionary mentor, and an inspirational political and philosophical provocateur and ally. They begin to suggest the range of Holt's life and interests.

Many essayists describe finding Holt through his writing and thinking as a kind of "king of renegade philosophers" as Alec Clowes says, or as a psychic and intellectual life preserver for Peter Bergson or Thomas Armstrong at a moment when they were young and ungrounded. Many speak about discovering Holt almost by chance and about his subsequent dramatic role and impact of his thinking on others around them and themselves. Philosophers Roland Meighan, Wendy Prieznitz, and Aaron Falbel describe his influence on their thinking, and call out Holt's capacity to describe the role of fear in most conventional learning, and of Holt's Theory of Mind. For example, in Meighan's chapter he writes, "children do not learn effectively by having a teacher transplant their reality into the children's mind; children learn by building up their own reality from experiences they encounter." Holt's keen perception of the role of coercion in almost all conventional learning—that whether friendly or unfriendly it creates barriers to cognitive performance that are immutable and insurmountable—emboldens these essayists to be brave and adventuresome in their own learning and living and helps them see that school is an institution that essentially narrows children's intelligence and capacity for learning. The essays describe what Vita Wallace calls Holt's role in joyfully liberating learning from schools, and in articulating what learner-centered education—now a trope in some reform circles—might actually look like. All the essays speak to Holt's passionate belief and capacity to describe why learning is too powerful to be stopped, too deeply set in the DNA of human beings to be squelched, how children are "already lit lamps," to quote Holt (in Falbel's essay, Chapter 15) and how frequently school gets this wrong.

In the Priesnitz, Bergson, and the Kaseman essays we see something that appeals to many of Holt's admirers: his capacity to name injustices against children, and his real work as a political advisor and strategist to those who were trying to escape compulsory schooling, state by state and province by province beginning in the late 1970s. We see the revolution and lifeline to freedom that *Growing Without Schooling*, the magazine Holt founded in 1977, actually was; and in the essays of Theo Giesy, the Kasemans, and Jenny Wright, the very real help John Holt offered, as individuals bravely went off to home school their children. Holt frequently offered these essayists the courage and confidence to trust their own children, to respect their children (itself a somewhat countercultural notion), and therefore, truly, to respect themselves. As Holt frequently pointed out, schools were not failing, they were doing exactly what they were designed to do—to create passive and quiescent children and adults who believe what they have been told about themselves by others.

Ultimately, as many of these essayists point out, Holt's greatest and most passionate writing and influence were in the ways he described learning itself—the ways we engage in evasion and self-deception when we are not doing something we need to do, and the beauty and power of continuing on with learning, even when we're lost. (Aaron Falbel offers a critical clarification about Holt's philosophy: It is not that Holt thought learning was easy, it was simply that he thought human beings had a deep desire to learn that we often ignore.) As Roland Meighan's essay describes, the journey of learning is ultimately a self-guided one, a path lit by the wisdom of the student and not the teacher. Quoting Holt (1978/1991):

> But even while giving me this help, the teacher I need must accept that he or she is my partner and helper and not my boss, that in this journey of musical exploration and adventure, I am the captain. Expert guides and pilots I can use, no doubt about it. But it is my expedition; I gain the most if it succeeds and lose the most if it fails, and I must remain in charge. (pp. 216–217)

For Holt the learner as a courageous adventurer, the expeditioner, the one upon whom responsibility rests and ultimately falls—an image very much at variance with conventional schooling—is an image that is mirrored again and again throughout the essays.

Finally, many of the essays show Holt's philosophy of living: The importance he placed on enjoyment, simple pleasure, in the creation of a meaningful life, and of "not taking any shit" while you were doing it. If

Holt was "a king of renegade philosophers," he was also strong as an ox in his youth, and a fearsome swearer; the essays offer a real sense of Holt as a physical presence and an assessment of Holt's life that is both admiring and wistful. As Kirk Talbott says,

> . . . he followed a path that was as authentic and original as any I have ever known. Perhaps his greatest legacy is reflected in the fact that both those who knew him intimately and the thousands who knew him from a distance through his words and ideas have been so deeply touched and moved in their own lives.

Or Peggy Hughes remembers Holt's great enjoyment in watching a seven-year-old boy in Denmark, who stood at the top of an escalator in a department store by himself, and was greeted with great dignity and respect by all passing adults. There is longing here in many of the essays—as there is in many marginalized movements—for a Great Man who could come along and score the knock out punch to the mainstream that would finally and fully legitimize the underdog movement's point of view. But as Wendy Priesnitz points out powerfully, Holt had no interest in being a guru, and even less desire to establish a school or create a set of philosophical points for others to follow. If one wanted to be a "follower" of Holt, the very point was one had to step up to own one's learning and to chart one's own path, to engage fully in the difficult and confusing business of sorting out what was meaningful to one's self, and to live fully and completely into this.

HOLT AS A WRITER

Many who write about education do so without paradox, without a capacity for perspective-taking, without a sense of refined intelligence underneath simplicity that makes Holt worth reading—whether you agree with him or not. Holt advanced and enlarged his political philosophy and educational ideas not only through writing books, but also in voluminous letter writing, visiting, and public speaking. One of the ways Holt distinguished himself from other critics of his era was the simplicity and elegance of his observations of learning, in his capacity for the straightforward yet evocative metaphor, and in the disciplined life force that lies below many of his sentences and ideas. So another of the pleasures of this book are the Holt quotes highlighted by the essayists! Children in school are like, "convicts in a chain gang, forced under threat of punishment to move along a rough path leading nobody knew where, and down which they could hardly see more than a few steps ahead"; a child trying to follow math instruction as being like a tank driver, sightless, plowing blindly across a plain; school as prison; "the schools are not failing . . . they are doing what most people want them to do very well . . . the first task is to shut young people out of adult society" (Holt, 1976/2004, pp. 157–158).

Master of the profound thought in the plainly crafted sentence, many of the essayists describe Holt's influence on them as a writer. Holt worked very explicitly on not being fancy, on not becoming academic, on avoiding the hyperbole of many of his compatriot writers of the time. Several of the essayists here recall Holt's advice on their own writing. Thomas Armstrong remembers John Holt told him,

> that my writing was too intellectual, too bookish, too much of the university, and not conversational enough. He told me to write as if I was sitting across the cracker barrel from someone telling a story. I've tried to remember that advice ever since.

The famous editor Merloyd Lawrence called Holt's capacity for description like that of "a great naturalist," and that his simple, modest, and to-the-point book proposals, "stated that he would do exactly what he would do"—an unusual quality in any writer. And Wendy Priesnitz observed that Holt's plainspoken style, and "lack of conceit" while writing on critically important topics, ensures that his work will endure.

None of this is happenstance, of course; the simplicity of the style, its accessibility or captivating imagery. Holt observed about his own style, in a letter to A.S. Neill (quoted here by Vita Wallace),

> I am pleased that you find my style readable. I work very hard to make it that way. Nothing annoys me more about the academic-intellectual community than their notion that an idea is important in proportion as it is obscure. I feel a moral as well as an aesthetic duty to speak as plainly as I can. (cited in Sheffer, 1990, p. 114)

As Thomas Armstrong observes in this volume, coming back to reading Holt after some time away is to feel " . . . once again those clear cadences, those child-centered passages that felt like a burst of fresh air rushing into a congested room." Many readers of this volume may feel similarly refreshed, and wonder why Holt has been missing from their lives.

WHAT JOHN HOLT MEANS TO ME

My own battered copy of *How Children Fail* (revised edition, 1982), rescued from the discard pile of the Harvard Graduate School of Education library in the late 1990s, has so many multi-colored Post-Its, marginal scribbles, and written evidence of my own learning that the pages have become detached from its binding and are held together by a large purple rubber band. This textual monument to my learning, a book found during the height of internecine wars of No Child Left Behind (NCLB)—marks a critical moment for me in my life as a writer and graduate student.

As the NCLB wars raged around my fellow graduate students and me (or actually *didn't* rage, because most people willingly and somewhat unquestioningly accepted the precepts about learning that this law was about to exact), finding John Holt, for me, felt like discovering a true colleague, a brother, a mentor and a teacher. Here (at last) was a teacher with a vision broad enough and radical enough to keep me in graduate school, to convince me that other perceptive observers had surveyed the educational establishment long before me and understood what was wrong, and that perhaps a time might come again when the simple brilliance of his words and perceptions would be understood and appreciated. In the meantime, John Holt kept me company through graduate school: on trains from New Haven to Cambridge, as I fought with scholarly committees to do my qualifying paper on Holt, as I traveled around the country talking with students for research to undergird and inform my writing, and finally as I battled with advisors to write a dissertation on Holt and his colleagues—to the horror of most of the faculty who were sure I was consigning myself to an obscure and second-rate academic career by choosing so unpopular and "unzeitgeisty" a topic.

But as the essays in this volume describe, each in their own deeply personal way, once John Holt has entered your system and has given voice to many of your own perceptions—*only more clearly, more eloquently, more truthfully than you have formerly allowed yourself*—(becoming an education radical is a lot about giving one's self permission to be truthful), Holt will become a part of you. It becomes difficult to sort out what is you and what is him—except that his own deep individuality is so much a part of him that you cannot forget the man who played cello in the Boston Garden, who composted on his terrace and bathed in a small washtub because he was saving water, who refused conventional medical treatment for a malignant melanoma, who picked up the trash as he walked around Boston, who died too early, or who cried in Pat Farenga's office because he never found a wife.

The experience of reading John Holt for many of us is like arriving back at an old friend, a friend whom you didn't necessarily know you had, after journeying on the road for many long decades. As Susannah Sheffer notes in her beautiful, poignant essay in this volume about John Holt's influence on her own life—we are challenged, if we go to the far edges of our learning, to find important colleagues, to create a circle of voices and presences around us to help give us confidence on the journey. Often we have to go far to find these colleagues. In issue 60 of *Growing Without Schooling* magazine, an unpublished letter of John Holt (1971) reads,

> One might say that one of our important life tasks was to find our true teachers, to make our own university [. . .] Certainly to find one of one's own teachers, someone from whom we think we can learn something really important, is one of the really great pleasures of life. (p. 15)

Although I never met him, John Holt was for me a true teacher, one whom I am still exploring and enjoying, now through this colorful group of essays celebrating Holt's life and work.

To people who are passionately devoted to the pleasure and enjoyment of learning new and difficult things, Holt speaks eloquently about the kind of self-confidence required to go forward into the unknown, the kind of vulnerability and courage that *not-knowing* requires at an interpersonal level, and then the sheer fun of keeping at something that's hard, even if you're not very good at it. Holt was my own true teacher in this; he was my coach and colleague at the Harvard Graduate School of Education during a very lonely time when his books were not even in circulation at the library. I read him with a sense of coming home, and of being brought to my best self.

If you approach the work of John Holt not from the wounds that you may have encountered in school, and not as a long-time defender of educative processes that occur outside of conventional school, and look at him simply as a great practical philosopher, you will find an abundance of riches: a brilliant writing mind, a capacity for the observation of individuals involved in learning (something very rare and precious in the world of education), a philosopher's capacity to connect small, seemingly insignificant actions to a much larger and more important point of view about social change and social transformation. The essays in this volume speak to Holt's capacity to inspire others: To teach them that they are not as "trapped as they think they are," in the words of Susannah Sheffer, or that they should, "connect with their own inner strength and wisdom and do what they love," or that they might learn to be humble, circumspect, and kind when "engag[ing] meaningfully with people different from ourselves," which Pat Farenga learned from Holt. As Roland Meighan wisely observes in this volume,

> . . . the reception of Holt's message: unpopular, except with some, and still unpopular because as a culture we are not quite yet ready to admit that school is a toxic and largely dysfunctional and wasteful system, and that there might be much better ways to provide child care and community for children and young adults, if we would only allow ourselves the opportunity to think about the problem in this way.

The above passage is as intriguing now as it was in the 1970s. As learning around the world jumps out of school, now is the moment to reengage with Holt's messages.

References

Sheffer, S. (Ed.). (1990). *A life worth living: Selected letters of John Holt*. USA: Ohio State University Press.

Holt, J. (1971). Notes for talks to students. *Growing without schooling, 60*, 15.

Holt, J. (1982). *How children fail* (Revised ed.). New York, NY: Delta. (Original work published 1964)

Holt, J. (2004). *Instead of education: Ways to help people do things better*. Boulder, CO: Sentient Publications. (Original work published 1976)

Holt, J. (1991). *Never too late: My musical life story*. USA: Da Capo Press. (Original work published 1978)

Kirsten Olson is the author of *Wounded By School: Recapturing the Joy in Learning and Standing Up To Old School Culture* (Teachers College Press 2009), *Schools As Colonizers* (Verlag 2008), and the forthcoming *Mindfulness for School Leaders* (Corwin). A founding board member of IDEA, (the Institute for Democratic Education in America), an organization linking youth and Progressive educational activists, Kirsten works with teams and individual educational leaders doing transformational work in education. She lives in Brookline, Massachusetts.

Learner-Managed Learning

By Roland Meighan

MEETING JOHN HOLT

When I met John Holt at the Birmingham UK Railway Station he was easy to recognize since he was the only passenger carrying a cello. This somewhat unusual piece of luggage was an indication of the priority he put on his music in the later years of his life. He was speaking at various conferences around England and in between his speaking engagements he would return to our house and settle down to play.

My wife Shirley was an accomplished pianist and so she and John found common cause. Sadly, both died within a few years of each other—Shirley in 1981 and John in 1985, both victims of cancer. The world lost two exceptional talents during this period.

The most autobiographical of Holt's (1978/1991) books is *Never Too Late: My Musical Life Story,* and although it is mostly the story of his love affair with music, strands of information about other aspects of his life are woven into it. He tells us that he came from an almost non-musical family and therefore did not learn to play an instrument as a child. He had no regrets about this, for he noted how plenty of people he met who were compelled to learn an instrument in their youth had their love of music diminished and sometimes extinguished in the process.

He began to play the flute at the age of thirty-four. He switched to the cello at forty and played for two years. Few adults who have never played take up an instrument in middle age and least of all a bowed string instrument, since it is supposed to be the hardest to learn. At the age of fifty, he took up the cello again and also began to write about his experiences in the hope that his story might encourage other people, above all adults, who may have been told that they were too old to begin to play a musical instrument. By now, he saw the task of becoming a skillful musician as the most important remaining task of his life.

HOLT'S IDEAS

His book *Never Too Late* (1978/1991) recorded his experiences of becoming a musician, but was also another of his works about education, about teaching—especially self-teaching—and also learning, especially learner-managed learning:

> This is also a book about teaching, above all the teaching of music. Some music teachers have been enormously helpful to me [. . .] But for the most part I am self-taught in music, and this book is also about that self-teaching. Part of the art of learning any difficult act, like music, is knowing both how to teach yourself and how best to use the teaching of others, how to gain from the greater experience and skill of other people without becoming dependent on them. (p. 2)

John finishes this passage with a significant observation: "What we can best learn from good teachers is how to teach ourselves better" (p. 2).

Holt adopted this as his definition of good teaching. Inadequate teachers worked *on* children, keeping them dependent, whereas good teachers worked *with* children, encouraging them to teach themselves and become independent learners. Self-teaching involves a series of stages—trial and error, feedback, self-correction, satisfaction, and pleasure—when it is a success. *Never Too Late* had a central concern with exploration and discovery.

A few general bits of information about his biography appear throughout *Never Too Late*. His parents were quite well off so he had an easy and comfortable young life. As an adult he chose to live with very little money so that he could do work he believed in, initially in the peace movement. He managed to maintain his modest life style without many worries about money. The fact that he did not marry was a contributory factor, although he explains that this was not of his choosing. It just never happened as he had hoped. He mentioned a girl he liked and went out with, but she found someone else she liked better.

But he had sufficient money to be able to explore, enjoy, and make music. *Never Too Late* was, in part, an attack on fatalism, for he questioned the belief that what happens to us in the first few years of life determines what follows. He proposed, instead, that it is never too late, a message that has cheered many an adult since.

Another task Holt set for himself was to question a commonly held belief that becoming a competent musician required relentless external compulsion. This was an erroneous and a dangerous doctrine, he wrote.

And he denied that the task of becoming musical required forced exposure, coercion, and threat. He set out to combat the idea that any disciplined activity, like all music, can never grow out of love, joy, and free choice. Most of what had been written about musical education said this in one way or another. Holt (1978/1991) declared that this idea is not only mistaken, but dangerous; nothing is more likely to make most people ignore or even hate great music than trying to ram more and more of it down the throats of more and more children in compulsory classes and lessons:

> The idea is wrong in a larger sense; in the long run, love and joy are more enduring sources of discipline and commitment than any amount of bribe and threat, and it is only what C. Wright Mills called the "crackpot realism" of our times that keeps us from seeing, or even being willing to see, that this is so. (p. 5)

Never Too Late is the most personal of Holt's books, for it contains many detailed anecdotes and accounts of his life. We learn that John Holt went away to school at Exeter, USA and discovered the big band sound of Tommy Dorsey. He also joined the school Glee Club. Later he developed an interest in classical music. His musical autobiography develops in chapters titled *Stravinsky* and *Woody Herman and I Meet Beethoven*.

There was only one family member, Aunt Jessie, who could play an instrument—the piano—so when she was around, evenings could be given over to singing the songs that his aunt played on the large, black upright piano at his grandmother's house.

When he applied to join the Freshman Glee Club at college, he was rejected because his voice was deemed "foggy, throaty and wheezy":

> But it still makes me regretful, and angry, that when I found out, almost by accident, that I loved making music and wanted more than anything to make some more, a rich university, dedicated (so they say) to the higher things of life, could have found nothing better to do than slam the door in my face. (Holt, 1991, pp. 65–66)

Later he and some friends formed a barbershop quartet. They enjoyed a short life singing together and performing at parties. Then a key member moved on to get married. After that Holt purchased a guitar and it gave him great pleasure for several years. But when he began teaching, he had little spare time for playing and so gave the guitar to one of his nephews.

He spent some time in the navy before working full time at the New York office of World Federalists, an organization promoting world government. Then in 1952 he spent some time in England, returning to the United States in 1953 to begin teaching in Colorado, where he stayed for four years. His next move was to Boston where he lived out the rest of his life, teaching, lecturing, and writing. It was during his years in Boston that he took up the cello. His move to Boston was a matter of chance. A friend and his wife offered him use of an apartment for two years whilst they were away in Africa. Holt took up the offer and found Boston to his liking and settled there.

But the success of his first book, *How Children Fail* (1964/1982), led to invitations to lecture, and he also set to work on his second book. The cello was squeezed out of his life for a time.

JOHN HOLT ARRIVES . . .

The work of John Holt came to my notice in a rather unusual way. My first partner came home from her school with a copy of *How Children Fail* in 1968, as I recall. Shirley was a teacher of the younger children at one of the few Primary schools in the Midlands ever to try to take the Plowden Report ideas of a child-centered approach at all seriously, much to the incredulity of the other schools in the area. Wherever the "Plowden revolution" was later alleged to have taken place, I can report with some confidence that it was *not* in the Midlands, since I and my colleagues were in and out of the region's primary schools with our students on a regular basis. Here the Dick Turpin highwayman approach continued to hold sway—"stand and deliver." Indeed, the research done, such as the ORACLE project from the University of Leicester, indicates that it hardly took place anywhere, despite the assertions of misinformed tabloid journalists based on a few anecdotes—some rare but true, others rare and only partly true, and others invented.

Shirley's head teacher had asked all the teachers on the staff to read *How Children Fail* in preparation for a staff meeting to reflect on the work of the school in the light of John Holt's ideas. So Shirley read it and then I read it and then we faced up to it: What Holt had to say squared uncomfortably with our experience.

I was not to know where this incident would lead. Later, we would meet John Holt and have him stay with us in Birmingham whilst he was on a European lecture tour.

The central message of *How Children Fail* was stark: Most children fail in school and indeed, due to the model on which we set up school, could hardly do anything else. Most fail in the school and society-defined tasks of first learning the imposed curriculum and then passing the tests derived from it. That was a grim verdict in itself, although not a new one. A former Chief Inspector of Schools for England and Wales, Edmond Holmes, had come to similar conclusions about the first National Curriculum that he had spent thirty years trying to implement. His two books, *What is and What Might Be* (1911), and *The Tragedy of Education* (1913) described the results of such an approach. John Holt (1964/1982) went further and pointed to a deeper sense of failure:

> But there is a more important sense in which almost all children fail: Except for a handful, who may or may not be good students, they fail to develop more than a tiny part of the tremendous capacity for learning, understanding, and creating with which they were born and of which they made full use during the first two or three years of their lives. (p. 5)

Holt (1978/1991) tells us that he picked up his cello again in 1973:

> If I could learn to play the cello well, as I thought I could, I could show by my own example that we all have greater powers than we think; that whatever we want to learn or learn to do, we probably can learn; that our lives and possibilities are not determined and fixed by what happened to us when we were little, or what experts say we can and cannot do. In my work with the cello, I might also find out things about learning music that might help many other adults learn it, or whatever else they wanted to learn. [. . .] In short, my love for music now seemed joined to my love of teaching and to my deepest political concerns. The gap I had felt between my work and my hobby had disappeared. (pp. 185–186)

In his reflections on his own learning of the cello, many of Holt's ideas about effective learning are reinforced. The trouble with most teachers, whether of music or of anything else, is that they act on the false assumption that learning is the result of teaching and even, in many cases, that learning *can only* be the result of teaching. Consequently, there is often an angry reaction to the idea that students might find out for themselves and an even angrier reaction to the idea that they would be better off by so doing. It is not enough for them to be helpful and useful to their students; they need to feel that their students could not get along without them:

> All my own work as a teacher and learner has led me to believe quite the opposite, that teaching is a very strong medicine, which like all strong medicines can quickly and easily turn into a poison. At the right time (i.e., when the student has asked for it) and in very small doses, it can indeed help learning. But at the wrong times, or in too large doses, it will slow down learning or prevent it altogether. (Holt, 1991, p. 209)

Fellow musicians had also absorbed the myth, for when they asked him who his cello teacher was, and he replied that he was teaching himself for the time being, they were surprised, or indignant, or even angry. It follows that Holt's (1978/1991) definition of a good teacher will continue to surprise, cause indignation or even anger:

> But even while giving me this help, the teacher I need must accept that he or she is my partner and helper and not my boss, that in this journey of musical exploration and adventure, I am the captain. Expert guides and pilots I can use, no doubt about it. But it is my expedition; I gain the most if it succeeds and lose the most if it fails, and I must remain in charge. (pp. 216–217)

At this time, 1973, John Holt (1976/2004) was also working on his book *Instead of Education*. But his work on the cello was no longer neglected. He applied the advice of Matthew Arnold to "clear a space." In other words, he stopped doing some things that he enjoyed in order to give time to his music. These included sailing, swimming, camping, mountain backpacking, skiing, squash, tennis, and soccer. He reports no regrets, for he saw music as athletics, as a sport more difficult and fascinating than any other he had ever played. There was enough teamwork and split-second timing in playing in an orchestra as in any sport. It was also a limitless field for thought, invention, and experiment.

He also reduced his general reading. The huge stacks of magazines and books he had always read were drastically reduced in number, for he already had considerable understanding. In any case, he noted that he already had all the bad news he could stand.

Holt received considerable encouragement as a result of meeting Janos Starker, one of the world's greatest cellists. Some friends who lived in Seattle, invited him to visit when Starker was playing in a concert. When Holt arrived in Seattle, he found that a small party had been arranged with Starker in attendance. At the party he decided to keep a low profile, but Starker approached him saying, "Good evening, Mr. Holt." In the conversation that followed Holt mentioned his desire to take up the cello again. Janos Starker observed, "Well. It's extremely difficult for someone of our age to learn to play this instrument well, because we have to develop a whole new set of muscles, and a whole new set of coordinations. On the other hand, we have an advantage." Holt asked him to explain. "We can think up problems, and find solutions" (Holt 1978/1991, p. 179). This resonated with John Holt. If you want to do it you can do it, he concluded, and it *is* possible for an old dog to learn new tricks.

Holt's work and development as a musician continued up until his death. He was conscious that he had not encountered any limitations because of his late start in music. He remained convinced from his own experience that it was never too late: "If Nature has waiting for me up the road some kind of impassable barrier, she has so far given me no clear signs of it" (Holt, 1978/1991, p. 242).

Holt proposed that school, in collusion with the dominant parts of the culture in which it operated, actually *reduced* the intelligence of most children so that they came out after 15,000 hours or so of schooling less intelligent than when they went in. In *How Children Fail* Holt was concerned to show how he had come to this conclusion. More importantly, in his observations in classrooms he attempted to uncover the underlying mechanisms, or in the current educational new-speak, the nature of the delivery systems.

There is a terrible irony in re-reading John Holt's message. Most of the bad techniques he identified that were fostered in the private schools, in which he taught and did his observations and analysis, are those which raise children's fears, and produce learning which is fragmented, distorted, and short-lived. They have become the basic building blocks of the second National Curriculum for England and Wales as well as the United States' schooling system. Indeed, most schooling systems throughout the world show the same basic characteristics, as Clive Harber (2004) showed in his *Schooling as Violence*, a survey of the consequences of schooling across the world, and in his later book, *Toxic Schooling* (2009).

Holt contemplated writing a book entitled *How to Make Schools Worse* to document the regressive developments as they occurred. He founded the organization *Growing Without Schooling* (in press) instead. But it follows that we cannot expect to find much inspiration in the educational approaches of other countries. We have to start again.

He also demonstrated the failure of the ideas of the progressives about making school work better:

> They thought, or at least talked and wrote as if they thought, that there were good ways and bad ways to

coerce children (the bad ones mean, harsh, cruel, the good ones gentle, persuasive, subtle, kindly), and that if they avoided the bad and stuck to the good they would do no harm. (Holt, 1964/1982, p. 294)

As an example, he looked at the New Math and was unimpressed. What he saw was the old math rearranged in a different pattern. It was still cookbook mathematics, even if some of the recipes looked newer and more inviting. Holt proposed that children couldn't learn much of any use from cookbooks, new or old, because children do not learn effectively by having a teacher transplant their reality into the children's mind; children learn by building up their own reality from the experiences they encounter. This was how young children learn and why, in the early years, they are such prolific and successful learners, a theme Holt (1989) took up in his last book, *Learning All the Time*.

A second irony is that Holt has been labeled as a progressive himself and identified with the very ideas he sought to expose. There was, he maintained, no way to coerce children without making them afraid, or more afraid. Fear is the inescapable companion of coercion and its inescapable consequence. Progressive education merely tried to find a kindly way to coerce children—the learning remained teacher-directed in a place of required attendance. Holt proposed that we must reject, therefore, the idea of schools and classrooms as places where, most of the time, children are doing what adults tell them to do, if we are serious about *educating* them rather than *schooling* them.

JOHN HOLT'S ANALYSIS

The questions Holt set out to answer were these: How does this mass failure take place? What really goes on in the classroom? What are these children who fail, doing? What goes on in their heads? Why don't they make more use of their capacity?

His thinking began as a series of memos written in the evenings to a colleague and friend whose fifth grade class he both observed and taught during the day. Later he arranged these memos under four main headings that reflected the themes that had emerged during his observations. They were Strategy; Fear and Failure; Real Learning; and How Schools Fail.

Holt taught in private schools with reputations for high standards, and he was at pains to point out that his book was not about bad schools or backward children; indeed, almost the reverse. Parents were paying out good money to have their children attend these schools. To all outward appearances the schools and the children were successful. The harmful effects of the schooling in question were ignored, not least because they were somewhat subtle in their operation:

> Strategy deals with the ways in which children try to meet, or dodge, the demands that adults make on them in school. *Fear and Failure* deals with the interaction in children of fear and failure and the effect of this on strategy and learning. *Real Learning* deals with the difference between what the children appear to know or are expected to know, and what they really know. *How Schools Fail* analyses the ways in which schools foster bad strategies, raise children's fears, produce learning which is usually fragmentary, distorted, and short-lived, and generally fail to meet the real needs of children. (Holt, 1964/1982, pp. 6–7)

There were various strategies that emerged from Holt's observations. Some students resist any involvement at all because they do not want the embarrassment of making mistakes and learn to avoid it. Others attempt to find tricks to locate the right answer. They are the "producers" who focus on feeding their teachers the right answers that are so clearly prized above all else. They jump at right answers and if they fail, they fall back into despair or defeat. It does double harm if they do get right answers by their strategies:

> When a child gets right answers by illegitimate means, and gets credit for knowing what he doesn't know, and knows he doesn't know, it does double harm. First he doesn't learn, his confusions are not cleared up; secondly, he comes to believe that a combination of bluffing, guessing, mind reading, snatching at clues, and getting answers from other people is what he is supposed to do at school; that this is what school is all about; that nothing else is possible. (Holt, 1964/1982, pp. 248–249)

Others try to please the teacher, whether they have any clue as to the right answer or not, by waving hands in the air enthusiastically—provided at least several others, including some successful "producers," have their hands in the air too. A common strategy, Holt noted, was mumbling answers, for a teacher anxious to get a right answer will assume that anything that sounds close is meant to be the right answer. An associated strategy is guess and look:

> There was a good deal of the tried-and-true strategy of *guess-and-look*, in which you start to say a word, all the

> while scrutinizing the teacher's face to see whether you are on the right track or not. With most teachers, no further strategies are needed. (Holt, 1964/1982, p. 25)

A few children are thinkers who try to assess meaning and work for understanding despite the dominance of the right-answer culture. But teachers who have such a fixed idea of the answer they require do not help these children; they will dismiss answers offered which are logical or even alternative correct answers. The culture of right answers had another unhelpful tendency, which was to value the *Yes* and other positive answers more than the *No* and negative ones even when the information yielded was the same:

> This, of course, is the result of the miseducation, in which "right answers" are the only ones that pay off. They have not learned how to learn from a mistake, or even that learning from mistakes is possible. If they say, "Is the number between 5,000 and 10,000?" and I say yes, they cheer; if I say no, they groan, even though they get exactly the same amount of information in either case. (Holt, 1964/1982, p. 54)

Relief often followed a mistake, for correct answers create a strain and anxiety because more right answers are then expected. The consequence is a low tolerance of uncertainty in both teachers and taught, because answer grabbing and teacher pleasing take continual precedence over thinking and understanding.

Holt concludes that the results of all this are far from trivial. The strategies are defensive in attempting to avoid trouble, disapproval, loss of status, embarrassment, ridicule and other punishment. They are fear-laden and neurotic. They are self-limiting and self-defeating. In the process children's intelligence is destroyed and their behavior becomes more and more stress-laden. They are learning to behave stupidly in the school's temple of right answers, with the teacher high priests devoted to the doctrine of tell them and test them. Only the few determined thinkers can ride out this system and survive intact.

But from the children's point of view, their behavior is intelligent because it minimizes stress. They give up on thinking school will ever make much sense. The point is to survive each day with as much dignity intact as possible:

> For children, the central business of school is not learning, whatever this vague word means; it is getting these daily tasks done, or at least out of the way, with a

minimum of effort and unpleasantness. (Holt, 1964/1982, p. 38)

But this approach neither serves them well in the pursuit of the school's desires, nor does it develop their confidence as learners with understanding. Furthermore, it does not match the teacher's idea of taking the students on a journey to some glorious destination well worth the pains of the trip:

> So the valiant and resolute band of travellers I thought I was leading toward a much-hoped-for destination turned out instead to be much more like convicts in a chain gang, forced under threat of punishment to move along a rough path leading nobody knew where, and down which they could hardly see more than a few steps ahead. School feels like this to children: it is a place where *they* make you go and where *they* tell you to do things and where *they* try to make your life unpleasant if you don't do them or don't do them right. (Holt, 1964/1982, p. 38)

These false messages about learning are reinforced by tests. Tests are supposed to make children work harder. Holt disagreed. Since children tend to feel threatened by tests, they work worse, not better. Scared soldiers might be thought to fight better, but a scared learner is almost always a poor learner.

Tests are supposed to show what children have learned. But teachers everywhere need good test results as much as, if not even more than, the children to prove that they are good teachers. So tests are announced in advance and the type of contents outlined. Practicing and coaching in the kind of material to appear in the tests then follows. Students recognize the dishonesty of stressing and rewarding this shallow appearance of knowledge rather than working for real, deep understanding:

> In short, our "Tell-'em-and-test-'em" way of teaching leaves most students increasingly confused, aware that their academic success rests on shaky foundations, and convinced that school is mainly a place where you follow meaningless procedures to get meaningless answers to meaningless questions. (Holt, 1964/1982, p. 256)

From his observations, John Holt (1964/1982) provided three answers to the question of why children fail. "They fail because they are afraid, bored, or confused" (p. 5). These often occur in combination. Holt notes, "They are afraid, above all else, of failing, of disappointing or displeasing the many anxious adults around them, whose limitless hopes and expectations for them hang over their heads like a cloud" (p. 6).

They are bored because most of the things they are given and told to do in school are so trivial and dull. They make such limited and narrow demands on the wide spectrum of their intelligence, capabilities, and talents.

They are confused because most of the torrent of words that pours over them in school makes little or no sense. It often flatly contradicts other things they have been told, and hardly ever has any relation to what they already know—to the rough model of reality that they carry around in their heads.

Holt's impact was that of a growing and persistent exposure of the fallacies of day-prison schooling. It was not a popular message since day-prison schooling suits the officials who want to impose ideas on the young, suits most teachers who are trained to be the sage on the stage, and suits many parents who want somewhere safe to dump children and adolescents. Encouraging the young to be self-managed learners is not on their agenda.

HOME-BASED EDUCATION

Holt's general concerns for education began about this time to take a different form. He changed emphasis from giving his time to trying to improve schools to supporting home-based education, often referred to rather misleadingly as homeschooling:

> For many years, with many others, I tried to make schools more kindly, interesting, competent, and serious. It now seems clear that in the near future this will not happen, mostly because there are so few people, in or out of schools, who want it to happen. To those few people who can't stand what schools are doing to their children, I now urge that they look for ways to take their children out altogether and have them learn at home. To help them do this I have begun to publish a newsletter, *Growing Without Schooling*. (Holt, 1978/1991, pp. 240–41)

Holt's book *Never Too Late* received enthusiastic support from Sir Yehudi Menuhin, who was educated at home. Menuhin attended school for just half a day. In a July 1996 radio interview he explained:

Questioner: You never went to school? Or you did for one day?

Yehudi Menuhin: Not even one day; one morning. When I came back from the morning, my mother asked me what had I learnt. I said "I really didn't learn anything. I sat at the back of the class, and there was a little window high up on the wall through which I could see branches. I hoped that a bird would alight. No bird alighted, but I kept hoping." And that's about all I could report. So my mother promptly said, "Well, we'll educate you at home."

Menuhin wrote about *Never Too Late*:

Never Too Late is an altogether sympathetic, heart-warming book. John Holt has found the secret of youth, for his discovery that constant studying, thinking and trying, spell constant progress, constant growth and improvement, and are, in fact, the attributes of youth.

Of course, he loved music for a considerable time and kept alive his capacity and enthusiasm for and his attention to sounds and their creation.

I applaud this book heartily; may everyone reading it stay young, well and warm-hearted in the same way. (Source unknown.)

Until the end of his life, home-based education took over as Holt's major concern in education. My last conversations with John Holt before he left to return to the United States were about the idea of flexischooling. We had both encountered parents who thought that they could "get the best of both worlds" if they were able to negotiate a flexible contract with their local school. We thought we might be able to write a book together about this idea and the effects it might have on schooling, but with John's illness and death it fell to me to produce the book, *Flexischooling* in 1988.

References

Edmond, H. (2012). *What is and what might be?* Forgotten Books.org. (Original work published 1911)

Edmond, H. (1913). *The tragedy of education*. London: Constable and company.
Arber, C. (2009). *Toxic schooling: How schools became worse*. Nottingham, UK: Educational Heretics Press.
Arber, C. (2004). *Schooling as violence: How schools harm pupils and societies*. Abingdon, Oxon: RoutledgeFalmer.
Farenga, P., Ricci, C., & Tedesco, S. (Eds.) (in press). *Growing without schooling*. Medford, MA: HoltGWS LLC.
Holt, J. (1982). *How children fail* (Revised ed.). USA: Da Capo Press. (Original work published 1964)
Holt, J. (1991). *Never too late: My musical life story*. USA: Da Capo Press. (Original work published 1978)
Holt, J. (1989). *Learning all the time: How small children begin to read, write, count, and investigate the world, without being taught*. USA: Da Capo Press.
Holt, J. (2004). *Instead of education: Ways to help people do things better*. Boulder, CO: Sentient Publications. (Original work published 1976)
Meighan, R. (1988). *Flexischooling*. Ticknall, UK: Education Now Books.

Dr. Roland Meighan is an acknowledged Educational Heretic for his view that mass compulsory schooling is an obsolete, counter-productive learning system which abuses human rights and that it should be phased out as soon as possible. Schools should be recycled as part of a flexible learning system which is invitational and learner-directed. He is author of more than ten books and has been translated into twelve languages.

He is a Fellow of the Royal Society of Arts, Director of Educational Heretics Press, Director/Trustee of the Centre for Personalised Education Trust Ltd., and formerly Special Professor of Education at the University of Nottingham, UK.

Music Comes Naturally and Technique Can Come Later

By Vita Wallace

Although he died when I was only 10, John probably influenced the course of my life more than anyone else outside my family. John's newsletter, *Growing Without Schooling*, his books, correspondence, and friendship gave my parents the courage to take my brother, Ishmael, out of school in second grade and to keep me out altogether. Of course it's hard to know how my life would have unfolded had I gone to school, but I think that homeschooling helped me to remain an eager learner, very close to my brother, and comfortable with not necessarily "being normal." John also inspired and encouraged my brother and me as we were beginning to make music, and both of us are now professional musicians. John's ideas about music and learning definitely shape the way we teach, and though we don't think about it much, conversations around our dinner table with John and his friends probably also had a great deal to do with where and how and what we play.

I have many memories of John, but I don't remember our first meeting. I must have been four or five years old. Ishmael was miserable in first grade, so our parents, Nancy and Bob, were searching for help when they discovered John's books in the library. As we began homeschooling and encountered difficulties, Nancy wrote and called John, and he was generous with help and advice. We were living in an old house in New Hampshire, and John lived nearby in Boston. I almost remember him from when our family went to Boston to buy a violin. I heard a string quartet at an Apple Hill Chamber Players concert and found the shiny little violins just my size. I stood up on my chair, pointed at one, and said "I want to play *that!*" John recommended a violin shop, where I remember being measured (it turned out that I needed a 1/8 size). Afterwards we went to John's office and someone helped me label my new violin case with a gun that made white letters on black stickers. I guess that machine made more of an impression on me than John did! My first memories of John himself are from a visit that Ishmael described in his diary:

March 26. We drove to a bus stop and found John Holt. I had forgotten what he looked like. We drove him home and then drove to Apple Hill for Vita's first violin lesson. I found a copy there of Monteverdi's *Orfeo* (the orchestral and vocal score). We drove home. After a walk and supper, Nancy and John played their Vivaldi Cello Sonata (John brought his cello) and we all improvised on different instruments.

March 27. After breakfast we lazed around and rehearsed "Cabbie." We had decided to surprise John with it as well as pancakes for breakfast. The rehearsal went very well and then we did a performance. Then I did part of a piano lesson and Vita and John improvised on the cello and violin. I practiced some Purcell with Bob, who played the recorder. The piece was called "Pipes are Sweet on a Summer's Day." Then I improvised on John's cello and played the Purcell again with Bob. After lunch—but I'd better explain. John Holt had written down a tune to Blake's "The Divine Image," in his own notation, consisting of each line representing a half step. We (him, me, and Nancy) spent almost the whole time deciphering and translating this tune. We used the rest of the time for going on a walk and having a snowball fight. We didn't quite get the tune down, but we got a good sketch of it. We had supper and a family concert. We named ourselves "The Bedchamber Players." The next day we brought John to the bus stop and he went off.

I remember my excitement as we formed The Bedchamber Players. We had a green upright piano in the kitchen, but our great-grandmother and great-grandaunt's Knabe grand piano was in John's "bedchamber," where we were gathered. John proposed the name and we all whooped with glee! I thought that having John stay with us, messing about with us, was the most fun thing ever—it felt like having a helium balloon in the stomach!

I don't know whether John introduced jam sessions in our family or whether we'd been improvising together already, but they were a great way for me to play with John and with the family. I only knew a few pieces on the piano and couldn't read music yet, so I sometimes felt left out even when our family sang around the piano, but from the beginning, John encouraged me to play "fire engines" up and down the violin and "play like the pros," fearlessly and with flourishes. We improvised "knock-knock sonatas" together, beginning with two knocks on the wood of the violin or cello and continuing with musical questions and answers. He was an exciting musical playmate, though I remember being bored by his endless careful tuning of his cello. He didn't seem to have the sense that anything was impossible to do or learn and he encouraged us to learn by just doing.

I loved listening to John's stories of living on a submarine during World War II, traveling all over the world, and hearing and meeting "the pros" at Boston Symphony Orchestra (BSO) concerts. I loved his jokes ("Der iceman bringt ein piece von decent size" and "Der vindow Viper") and his songs ("When ducks get up in the morning, they always say good day"). He had a beautiful voice and he whistled really well, too. From my point of view, he was nice and cushy to sit on or lean against and he wore nice-smelling wool sweaters. He loved to eat, and if he caused Nancy extra work by staying and eating with us for days and days, at least he exclaimed over every dish.

I remember two meltdowns I had while John was visiting. The first was a temper tantrum. I was lying on the kitchen floor kicking and screaming because we had taken the dirt road home from the cemetery instead of walking through the woods and fields and climbing on my favorite mossy boulder. Since I hadn't gotten my way, I wanted to be miserable and misunderstood, the more miserable the better! John was standing over me murmuring that he understood how I felt. How annoying! A few years later in our new house in Ithaca, NY, I started crying over my math book, which claimed that to divide fractions you had to turn one upside down and multiply. Never mind that you got the right answer that way, it seemed to me to be some kind of ridiculous trick, and it just didn't make any *sense.* John, lying on the couch, quietly started figuring out *why* it worked with a pencil and paper. This time I appreciated his calm reasonableness. I can't remember his explanation any more, but I dried my tears, and it's still a comfort to me to know that I understood it once.

I remember waiting for John to arrive at our house in Ithaca in time for a late supper—the excitement of anticipation and sneaking an elbow noodle from the macaroni salad now and then. Nancy played the viola, I was beginning to read music, and our father was beginning to study the cello; it must have been John's idea for the five of us to play the Mozart "G Minor Piano Quartet." Was it ever too hard for us! Except perhaps for Ishmael. I've just performed it for the first time and I had the wonderful experience of "learning it from memory," because we must have listened to it over and over again. Back then, however, even though I had a special part with only one note per measure, I was completely lost and just sat there next to Nancy on the chest that was our coffee table, listening to Ishmael spinning out strings of pearly notes. Ishmael shot ahead of the rest of our family musically and soon he and John were working on the Beethoven "A Major Cello Sonata." The opening melody of the first movement brings John right back to me, warm and searching.

Perhaps John was on the couch the time he helped me with fractions because his cancer was already making him weak, but he had always liked naps. I remember bouncing around the house in New Hampshire full of the excitement of having him there, restraining myself with difficulty from running into the guest room and waking him up. He could also fall asleep sitting up, right in the middle of a conversation, which I thought was very funny. He told me that once he fell asleep standing on the court in the middle of a basketball game!

John was also sweetly vulnerable in another way. In reading his letters and his book *Never Too Late* (1978/1991), I'm struck by the number of times he says he's burst into tears listening to music, reading a book, or looking at a view. I remember him crying while reading us a poem in Ithaca, "Not Marble Nor the Gilded Monuments" by Archibald MacLeish (1985). I thought the poem reminded him of a girl he was in love with years before, but I may not have understood what was going on, because Ishmael says that John was reading us the poem in order to let us know that though he would die soon, a part of him would remain with us. No wonder he was crying!

Shortly after John's death, I had an experience that struck me very much. It was at a rehearsal of our Area All-State High School Orchestra, which I was allowed to join even though I was too young and didn't go to school. The conductor was one of the assistant conductors of John's beloved BSO, Carl St. Clair (he was a truly wonderful teacher). When I heard that I had been chosen to play principal second violin, I rushed out of the hall to tell John. I knew exactly where he was—but just when I expected to run into him, I stopped, bewildered. I saw only a sunbeam where he ought to have been.

I think of John often, when I tune using harmonics, sound out a perfect fourth using "Here Comes the Bride," or give 50 cents to anyone who asks, all of which I learned from him. (John gave a quarter, but that was a long time ago.) Ishmael and I have lived in New York City for over 15 years now. I feel very lucky that Ishmael and his wife, Marleenee, live upstairs from me. In addition to our work together as the Orfeo Duo, I play early music and Ishmael coaches singers and composes. We've been lucky enough to make a lot of recordings together, most recently the Beethoven violin sonatas on period instruments (speaking of not worrying too much about "being normal," we didn't edit those recordings). When that was done I jumped into playing swing music on the accordion and old-time fiddle tunes, and Ishmael started singing seriously!

Our main focus since 2003, however, has been developing a wonderful more-than-a-concert-series called *What a Neighborhood!* which celebrates Morningside Heights and West Harlem (the area within walking distance of our home) primarily through the music of local composers. Our goals for the project are to encourage and inspire composers and other neighbors, develop grassroots support for new American music, and draw neighbors together, nurturing a sense of community that includes all of the diversity of our area. We experiment and explore, collaborate and create, cultivate and celebrate with lots of neighbors each year. Recent events have included meditation, storytelling, musical seances, family dances, and singing walks. We lead weekly jam sessions at a soup kitchen as well as lots of other composition, improvisation, and chamber music workshops. (If you'd like, you can read more about it all on our website, www.orfeoduo.com.)

Every time we teach we return to John's philosophy that making music comes naturally and technique can come later. We have led innumerable jam sessions with people of all ages and backgrounds; we know that it's fun for the participants partly because the two of us have a lot of experience, but at the same time we enjoy being reminded by them of the joy and the healing power of making music. We stress that even if they don't have any musical education they really are making music, and we show them that they have a lot of unconscious knowledge. We also teach composition with a strong emphasis on listening to one's inner voice, not worrying about notation. Though we are fascinated by the ins and outs of different musical styles, we don't believe that some styles are more worthy than others. We also don't believe that classical music or avant-garde new music can only be enjoyed by *cognoscenti*. We constantly strive to play music as an expression of the breath of life and to present classical music as a form of human expression that people can both relate to and be inspired by.

I didn't know that John had actually thought about and worked on some of the same issues until I recently discovered this passage from 1971 in *A Life Worth Living: Selected Letters of John Holt,* edited by Susannah Sheffer (1990):

> As you know, I am a classical music freak. I have been associated with a small orchestra here in Boston called the Philharmonic, of which I have become a trustee and am now a vice president. I am interested in finding ways to get a whole lot of people to go to concerts who have never been. Also, the conductor of the Indianapolis Symphony is a dear friend of mine and an absolutely wonderful man and musician, and I am concerned how to help him and his organization grow. I expect I'll be more into this in the next couple of years, trying to broaden the audience for classical music and indeed others of the arts. All of this seems to me to fit very closely with what Illich is writing about. The liberation of learning—actually that's my phrase—from the confines of schools. (p. 91)

As Ishmael says, it is part of John's wider philosophy, which he probably discovered for himself and then had confirmed by Ivan Illich, that people have wisdom and can access it without it being given to them, or sold to them, by schools or experts.

In the same edited collection, another of John's letters, to A. S. Neill in 1972:

> I am pleased that you find my style readable. I work very hard to make it that way. Nothing annoys me more about the academic-intellectual community than their notion that an idea is important in proportion as it is obscure. I feel a moral as well as an aesthetic duty to speak as plainly as I can. (p. 114)

I don't usually think of our work as political, but the choices we have made about what and where and how to play, and with whom, reflect a certain outlook on life and an attempt to "be the change we wish to see in the world" in our own neighborhood. Here's another quote from one of John's letters, from 1975:

> Actually there is a very important political component in my cello, and if I hadn't seen it or invented it, I would probably not be able to justify spending the four to six hours a day I am now putting in on it. My point is that modern society makes people feel powerless. I keep thinking of the distinction that Erich Fromm made between potency and dominance. People seek dominance over other people, or identify themselves with dominators, because they don't feel potent, capable of doing things, changing things. I would like to demonstrate that it is possible for somebody of 50 years of age to do something that *all* the experts say is flatly impossible, which is to become a really highly skilled musician. If I can do so, I think the point could be extended to a great many fields other than music. (cited in Sheffer, p. 187)

Making music seriously, year after year, naturally isn't all fun. Every day we have to face ourselves when we practice. Of course John's inspiration and our homeschooling didn't make us immune to self-doubt, worry about the unimportant stuff, and other troubles, and we frequently lose touch with our inner strength and wisdom. We're lucky to have each other and other friends who help us to find them again. Our work also reminds us what we love and what we believe is important. It's helpful to help others. A lot of our work stems from a desire to inspire and encourage people the way John inspired and encouraged us—not only to inspire people to make music, but to encourage them to connect with their own inner strength and wisdom and do what they love. I was tickled pink (as John would say) by something our Aunt Miggles once told us: "Your playing makes me feel like going out and doing things!"

References

Holt, J. (1991). *Never too late: My musical life story*. USA: Da Capo Press. (Original work published 1978)

MacLeish, A. (1985). *Collected poems 1917–1982*. Boston, MA: Houghton Mifflin.

Sheffer, S. (Ed.). (1990). *A life worth living: Selected letters of John Holt*. USA: Ohio State University Press.

Vita Wallace is a musician who was homeschooled until she turned 17. She is the daughter of the writer Nancy Wallace. Vita lives in New York City and is a member of the early-music ensembles Anima, ARTEK, the Dryden Ensemble, the Lyra Consort, and Foundling, as well as the new-music group Praxis. She and her brother, Ishmael, have performed, recorded, and taught extensively as the Orfeo Duo. For the past ten years, they have directed a series of concerts, workshops, and other gatherings called *What a Neighborhood!*, celebrating the creative spirit in Morningside Heights and West Harlem primarily through the music of living local composers. Vita loves gardening and creating situations in which friends, neighbors, and other artists can bloom.

King of the Renegade Philosophers

This is an edited version of a conversation Pat Farenga and Carlo Ricci conducted with Bud, Strobe, and Kirk Talbott, and Alec Clowes.

The Talbott family knew John Holt before he became a schoolteacher and he practically became a member of their family over time. Indeed, as you will read here and in Berrien Moore's essay, the Talbotts have a habit of "adopting" people into their family. Nelson "Bud" Talbott, an outdoorsman and conservationist, describes his friendship with John and how their bonds grew tighter over the years through camping trips. Prior to meeting Bud, John served in the U.S. Navy in World War II, as a lieutenant on a submarine in the Pacific—the USS Barbero. *After the war, John worked with the World Federalists, a group dedicated to creating a global government structure to prevent nuclear war.*

Bud Talbott: John Holt walked into my office in Dayton, Ohio and introduced himself and said he was working for the United World Federalists and that he had my name and that he would like to get acquainted. I took him out to the house—he was glad to accept a free night—and we just struck up a friendship right then. I thought it was terrific that he was doing what he was doing, because I had founded the United World Federalists chapter in Dayton, so John was doing that work with very little compensation, I am sure, but he travelled around the country and that was what he was doing in those days.

Pat: Can you give us a little background on who the World Federalists were and what their goals were?

Bud: It was quite active at one point in late 1940s and early 1950s and it still is around. The organization is called "The World Federalist Movement—Institute for Global Policy." Norman Cousins, the editor of the *Saturday Review of Literature*, was the intellectual leader of it. Katherine Meyer, who was very active in it, then joined the Kennedy administration. She later became the publisher of the *Washington Post*, as Katherine Graham. It was one of those organizations that was a little ahead of its time. I guess Katherine Meyer went out with Adlai Stevenson, who was a presidential candidate at one time. He was the young hero sportsman, he had a war record in the marines and what not.

There were chapters around the country and they were very much promoting the United Nations at the time of its formation.

John left the World Federalists a few years later, but my friendship with John continued and was robust over the years. He went on a number of camping trips in the summer with my kids and Alec Clowes. These included trips into the Algoma country north of Sault Ste. Marie in Canada, canoe trips in the Superior Quetico in Minnesota. I remember on the Minnesota trip we were camped on an island when a tornado front moved through. Strobe had been carrying my tent in his backpack and it apparently dropped off at the airport, so John and I had to fashion a tarpaulin, and John suggested we build the great Panama Canal to by-pass the rain deluge that was coming at us. It was a memorable night.

We also went into the Wind River Range in Wyoming on a number of occasions. These were backpacking trips, and John was always in good enough shape to climb up the mountains with a backpack on his back. I can remember, particularly, one night when we first went into the Wind River Range up in the mountains on a very clear night to watch the satellites, which was a relatively new phenomenon arcing across the sky, and also sitting under the magnificence of the Milky Way and all of the heavens.

Alec Clowes: I consider myself to be a member of the Talbott family and Bud to be my second father. He is really a very special person in my life, and camping was an important part of what we did together. The very first camping trip I went on was with John Holt when I was 10 or 12.

Bud: Well, the camping trips go back to when my mother and father spent their honeymoon at this camp up at mile 41, which was the early centerpiece of our trips. Then after that we spread out. That's right, Alec. You were on the first trip and maybe that was the first trip for John Holt.

Alec: That trip is vivid in my memory—we arrived and had to hike about a mile or a mile-and-a-half from the railroad whistle stop into the Pine lakes and then paddle in our canoes to the cabin. We arrived at the cabin and we had to shake out the mattresses where mice had set up housekeeping. That evening, or one of the early evenings, we watched a magnificent display of the aurora borealis. The sky turned bright green. John, at that time, was not married to his cello. He was married to a flute and stood out at the end of a dock and started playing. I remember John and the loons competing with one another to fill that sky with sound. It was a remarkable thing. It was magical.

Bud: I remember that very well.

Alec: I think I was 10 years old. That was not the very first trip you made up there because that was the one with Berrien. So it was either 1956 or 1958—somewhere in there.

Bud: I remember that the two of you were gung ho to shoot a squirrel with a pistol.

Alec: Strobe, do you remember that little adventure? Out of sight of John, who made scathing remarks, we did get a squirrel, and we tried to cook it. I think we wound up eating raw squirrel.

Kirk Talbott: John was really kind and would look me up and go out to dinner with me when I was at Yale. John played the cello and William Sloan Coffin played the piano over brandy or some drinks in the evening a couple of times. John was starting to get into worms. He would grow worms on his patio in Boston. He was always doing these crazy things, along with weight lifting. He was one strong son of a gun. Carrying those canoes though, he would get his shirt off and be sweaty and start swearing up a storm. He'd throw a canoe and a Duluth pack on his back and charge through the woods.

Bud: We had these twerpy little kids—Alec Clowes and Strobe—so we had to have an ox in the way of John Holt to carry the canoes.

Strobe Talbott: Bud, I think you were pretty good at finding the niches on our packs and putting the next can of baked beans or whatever into them until I felt like I was going to get driven into the ground. That's what I remember. I started out at the railroad headed to the lake and I think I barely made the first step.

By the way, Alec mentioned scathing remarks. One of the great things about John was his sense of humor. I do not think I have ever known a naturally funnier human being, although, of course, he was also a human being capable of the most serious contemplation and he had a huge intellect. And very sentimental in a lot of ways, but also contrarian. In fact, sometimes his contrariness and his sense of humor went together. You know, he loved to sort of debunk sacred cows, such as Shakespeare. For some reason it sticks in my mind. I remember conversations around the campfire at night where he made the case that Shakespeare was way over-rated as a literary figure. The kind of stuff that would have us scratching our heads, but then he would make the case, you know. An iconoclast, and he fell in love with Iceland at one point. I do not know if he ever went there.

Pat: He did.

Strobe: He decided he had had it with the United States and Iceland was the place to live. Does anyone remember that?

Alec: I do, but that was much, much later. I think that that was during the period of the Vietnam era where he was really fed up with the country.

Pat: I think that's right. But John decided there were more possibilities, more loopholes as he told me, in the United States for living and learning as he wanted, so he decided not to become an expatriate. Strobe, you stayed with John when you were translating *Khrushchev Remembers* (1970). Can you tell us a little about that?

Strobe: Well, I put it this way. My wife and I—let's see that was 1970, she wasn't yet my wife but she was visiting me in 1970 when I was in Boston and John offered to have us come over and stay at one point, and his apartment was such a mess that she did not want to spend the night there. What I remember is paper, dust, barbells, and musical stuff. Just total, total mayhem. And we went . . .

Alec: Real bachelor's pad.

Strobe: I'll say—and very uninviting for the female of the species.

Alec: Subterranean, if I remember, Strobe, on Chestnut Street. You had to walk down into it. It was rough and gloomy.

Strobe: We always had fun with him. He would always let us take him out to dinner and—I stress—let us take him out to dinner. I do not think John Holt ever picked up a tab.

Bud: You know that apartment. The recollection I have of that apartment was just before he died. He really went back to that apartment to die.

Strobe: Is that right? I thought he moved in with some friends, didn't he?

Pat: Yes, he had friends take care of him while he was receiving treatment.

Bud: And a woman from England came over.

Pat: Yes, Leila Berg.

Bud: To take care of him. It was very heart-rending experience for me to see him there and realize that he was going. I had never heard of this woman before, but John picked up people that appreciated him, I think, all his life.

Strobe: Including kids, which of course is a very important part of the story. If you guys are including pictures in this book, I have got two—I have one of John playing the cello and my son Devon, who was then maybe two, playing on a little kiddie flute. But he was just wonderful with kids and they just related to him so powerfully.

Alec: The other picture, Strobe, that ought to be in there is the one on the back of *How Children Fail* (1964/1982), his first book—the one in which he is mesmerized by all the Talbott kids falling all over one another trying to catch a frog. They all invariably got wet.

Strobe: It is actually Kirk who is holding the frog, right Kirk?

Kirk: As a 4 year old with my bullfrog, Jumpy.

Alec: I remember very well when that book was published. John, I think, had been at the Commonwealth School at that point, and he was a bit tentative about his ideas, He was unsure that anyone was listening or going to listen to him.

Bud: John's predilection for learning by doing was part of his character, and he was always taking the tack of being out in front. Each challenge presented an opportunity to address it in a sustainable and imaginative way. It was just part of his persona.

John's achievements as an educational reformer really came on quietly. In the 1950s, he apparently had some frustrating experiences when he was teaching in Colorado, being ahead of his time. He talked occasionally about teaching in school, but most of our conversations were very wide-ranging.

My thoughts about John in the 1960s were not different. I visited him in his office, and we tried to keep in touch as much as possible. I did feel that John was energized and glad to have notoriety and feel that he was making a contribution in the teaching profession. I continued to think of him as a fiery rebel. I certainly did not believe that *Growing Without Schooling* was in any way inconsistent with what he always had been standing for.

Pat: Did he strike you as a teacher when you first met him or was he just John?

Alec: No, he struck me as a king of renegade philosophers. I had some experiences with John in which I had some question about his interactions with children. I think he viewed children as a sort of a project. For example, we were traveling to Pinedale in Wyoming and were at the Denver airport. I vividly remember John sitting beside me. A mother came by and was in a rush to get to a plane. She had a little toddler who was busy inspecting every little nook and cranny. She finally, in frustration, bundled this squawking kid up in her arms and off they went. John was furious. He was about to charge after this woman and read her Miranda rights because she was abusing this child. He couldn't be calmed down for a whole hour after that. This sort of highlighted his somewhat idealistic but somewhat impractical view of life. We all adored him for that, but nevertheless sometimes it created awkwardness.

Pat: It's interesting you say that because, particularly in the 1960s and 1970s, he was pretty much known as a sort of a radical or maverick school reformer. When I met him he had really toned all that down by the 1980s; he said that he didn't think that arguing was an effective way to effect social change.

Strobe: I did not know that. My sense was that he bounced from one school to another. The Fayerweather School in Cambridge, The Commonwealth School, The Rocky Mountain School, and so forth. It's pretty much my recollection, and I am probably exaggerating it, but he always would depart, not under a cloud, but because he was not, shall we say, comfortable in an authoritarian environment or an orthodox environment. So he was always trying to push things and test things farther than the powers that be at any particular school wanted to go.

Pat: *How Children Fail* (1964/1982) was rejected by many publishers before it got published. Did you notice any despair in John during this period of his life? You noted how happy he was when it got published.

Alec: I remember that he was worried about it and hoping that somebody would be willing to publish it. He was confident in his ideas but he wasn't confident the world was going to pay any attention to what he was saying.

Strobe: I would say that John had a streak of melancholy in him, but he did not indulge it very much and despair, I would say. We all feel it sometimes, but he was very determined, very sure in his views, sure in his enthusiasms whether it was music and, most of all, of course, in his view of the world which was, I mean, "left" doesn't even do it. It was more than left because he had a lot of complaints with the traditional left, but of course, one of the most important things to him was friendship. There was a period there, Bud and I were recollecting this the other day, when he actually dropped off the camping trips for a year or two on the grounds that he did not feel that he could afford to go 10 days or 8 days without practicing his cello everyday.

Alec: Exactly. In fact I remember him traveling to Pinedale with us, but he refused to go into the mountains because he would have to leave his cello behind.

Bud: And he had a special backpack for his cello. John was a wonderful friend and a companion on those trips.

Strobe: Oh, you bet.

Bud: His sense of humor was wry and low-powered in some ways, but always right there; he was a joy to be with, although he obviously had some problems with relationships. He fell very much in love with a girl in Denver. But she just couldn't take his idiosyncrasies. I think he was sad down deep that he was not able to find a soul mate for himself. And though he picked up all of these friends over his lifetime, I always felt sad about that, because he was such a nice human being. But with his extreme views, you can certainly understand that a woman who wanted to have a comfortable conventional life wasn't going to get it with John.

Pat: Can you give us an example or tell us a story of John's sense of humor or wit?

Strobe: He had a stand-up comedian's sense of timing. I remember once Alec and I for some extremely sensible reason were in a canoe right off the pier at lower Pine lake and we were facing each other; that is, I was sitting in the stern facing forward and he was sitting in the bow facing backwards, and we were paddling like crazy and thought that was hilarious because, of course, the effect was to make the canoe just spin around in the water. Holt walked down to the end of the pier and watched this with this kind of mock-pensive look on his face, and shouted out to us, "Write when you get work."

Pat: You all describe John as a bit eccentric. Can you expand on that a little bit?

Alec: I always remember him being that way. You can even go back to the time of our camping—we would invariably rough it a bit. John would tell us stories from his submarine days, such as how to take a shower with a cup of water. He would then do it, even if we weren't in a submarine. I remember driving through central Michigan with Bud. Bud and I would often hold the late night shift. We would drive from about midnight until about three in the morning, having long conversations, and John would be splayed out diagonally in the back snoring away, with Strobe on one side and maybe somebody else on the other side—he would occupy an awful lot of space. And again, not being malicious, but sort of oblivious of what else was going on around him.

John was always enthusiastic, although he had a bit of a short fuse. I remember another trip we were on in which we were travelling between lakes—we had to bushwhack. I remember John with a canoe and a huge pack on his back, behaving like a giant rhinoceros plowing through the woods, cussing his way to success—it was unbelievable. So at times, even though he was an intellectual, he would resort to real physical approaches to getting on in life. I do not think he was ever a violent person, but when it came to dealing with nature, sometimes he got a bit rough.

Bud: And cursing up a storm.

Pat: Did John ever talk about teaching and school with you when he was on these camping trips?

Alec: Only in the sense that he would talk about the virtues of homeschooling. I think an abiding principle for John was that you had to get out of the way of the kid and let the kid discover his or her self. You should not put barriers in the way, and you should allow the child to explore the world with complete freedom. Anything you did that was conventional or that put a limitation on the child was not good. He would keep making this point in a thousand ways. It was fundamental to his homeschooling idea. That principle was evident from earliest days and he just elaborated on it over and over again.

Pat: That's very interesting that you always saw that there. So there wasn't a conversion moment for him, it was just something that was in him and that just kept getting stronger?

Alec: Well, it was evident from the time that I first met him, which was when he was at the Commonwealth School.

Pat: Both of you met John before he became a successful author and a well-known education reformer; did success change him in anyway?

Alec: I don't think so. Bud, what do you think?

Bud: I think just more so.

Alec: I do not think he was ever influenced by either fame or by dollars. I think he travelled his own path. John was initially interested in music, particularly the flute and then later on the cello. He used to talk to me about the Dvorak cello pieces. Did he ever explain to you, Pat, why he was so fond of Dvorak?

Pat: I do know that he listened to the Dvorak pieces a lot, but what I heard him practice a lot was Bach, the "Sarabande" in particular. John truly loved music. I remember sharing this with Bud when I met him in Boston after John passed away. The last two years of John's life he had made friends with a cellist with the Chicago symphony, David Chickering. And when John was dying Leila Berg came in from London, as Bud remembered, and then David came in from Chicago for John's last weeks. After the doctors said John would need hospice care and they couldn't do anything more for him at Massachusetts General, he just wanted to go home. I arranged to have nurses at his condo, but the nurses were very unreliable. So Leila, David, some other families, and I would spell each other while we cared for John. The day that John passed away David called me and told me the bad news. I came down to John's condo and it was such a beautiful moment for me, because as I was walking along the sidewalk and entering the apartment I could hear that beautiful "Sarabande" being played by David Chickering on John's cello; it was just gorgeous. I opened the door and there he was, next to John's body, playing that song. I just thought it was such a fitting moment.

Alec: Pat, you wanted another example of John's quirkiness. The very fact that he died of melanoma was due to his quirkiness. John himself was in denial, first of all, that he had a problem, then he decided he'd find nonconventional approaches to treating himself. I was greatly troubled by his choices because in those days I was already engaged in medicine and knew a lot about this terrible disease. I thought the outcome was a tragedy and that in a sense he set the stage for his own demise.

Bud: As you know Alec, he decided that Linus Pauling's Vitamin C therapy was the thing to do. I am not sure what aspect of the conventional treatment he was unhappy with, but he left and the doctors, I am sure, told him that he was signing his own death warrant. But he did not want to believe them. He was taking big doses of vitamin C because Linus Pauling had promoted that and then he went to Maine. Anyway, we stopped off to see John in Maine and he was with a family [the Hughes family. See the chapter, "A Close Family Friend"—Eds.]. What was interesting was in the final days of his life people stepped forward to take care of him. So he was with a family there, and Strobe and I saw John. When we got in the car, Strobe just broke down totally.

Alec: I remember, because I think I phoned you guys from wherever I was and talked to John. I remember his voice was very weak, and when I hung up I was in tears. The way he handled his illness reflected his contrarian spirit.

Bud: You have to be mad at him for being so stubborn about that.

Kirk: John was marvelous about writing letters—corresponding and always responding. An almost lost art these days. Each letter meant something special to the recipient. He made the young and insecure feel as important as anyone else. John told me that in Boston he always had a pocket full of quarters to be able to give a single quarter to everyone who wanted help or a handout. I thought that was a marvelous approach and consistent with John's *dao*.

John smiled easily and often and could belly laugh with the best of them. I've been told that is the mark of a content and considerate person. Whatever the circumstances of his death, he owned his life as few could even dream of, and he followed a path that was as authentic and original as any I have ever known. Perhaps that is his greatest legacy as reflected in the fact that both those who knew him intimately and the thousands who knew him from a distance through his words and ideas have been so deeply touched and moved in their own lives.

References

Holt, J. (1982). *How children fail* (Revised ed.). USA: Da Capo Press. (Original work published 1964)

Talbott, S. (Ed). (1970). *Khrushchev Remembers*. Boston, MA: Little, Brown and Company.

Alexander W. Clowes, M.D. received his AB (cum laude) from Harvard College in 1968 and his M.D. (cum laude) from Harvard Medical School in 1972. During his general surgery residency, Dr. Clowes developed his interest in vascular biology and arterial wound healing. Dr. Clowes is a member of many scientific societies and has been particularly active nationally and internationally in vascular surgical research activities. He is a recipient of a MERIT award from the National Institute of Health. He is also associated with various civic causes, foremost of which was his involvement in building Seattle's first symphony hall.

Nelson "Bud" Talbott was John Holt's dear friend and an organizer for their camping trips. Bud graduated from Yale (1943), is a WWII veteran (lieutenant in the Navy), worked in business and investment banking, and is active on a range of boards. When John was a field director for The United World Federalists, he met Bud, who was Chair of the Dayton chapter.

Kirk Talbott graduated from Yale (1978), Georgetown law, and foreign service school. He has worked in environment, human rights, and development for his career and is a Visiting Scholar at the Environmental Law Institute.

Strobe Talbott assumed the presidency of the Brookings Institution in July 2002 after a career in journalism, government, and academe. His immediate previous post was founding director of the Yale Center for the Study of Globalization. Before that, he served in the State Department from 1993 to 2001, first as ambassador-at-large and special adviser to the secretary of state for the new independent states of the former Soviet Union, then as deputy secretary of state for seven years. Mr. Talbott entered government service after 21 years with *Time* magazine. As a reporter, he covered Eastern Europe, the State Department, and the White House, then was Washington bureau chief, editor-at-large, and foreign affairs columnist.

We Drag Mathematics About until Everyone Is Put to Sleep

This is an edited transcript of a conversation between Pat Farenga and Dr. Berrien Moore.

Berrien Moore met John Holt through the Talbott family—Bud Talbott is his uncle through marriage—and they became very close over the years. Berrien's father died when he was 25 and Bud stepped in and became a close personal friend and a father figure—Bud was the best man at Berrien's wedding. Berrien first met John Holt when he was 11, but he didn't get to know John well until they went camping when Berrien was finishing graduate school in the late 1960s.

Berrien: There was a tit-for-tat between Bud Talbott and John Holt sometimes. For instance if the weather started turning bad Bud might say, 'Oh well, don't worry about it. The weather won't be that bad.' And John would take the position, "Let's get the hell out of here."

John enjoyed being in the wilderness, and he loved the camping trips, but why did he love the trips? I think it was because there was a group of young people sitting around a fire, away from telephones and society and its "rules."

I think that his enjoyment of Rachel Carson was the fact that she fundamentally questioned the norms of the day as opposed to his having some great love of the wilderness or bird watching or fishing or nature. John clearly enjoyed and was comfortable with nature, but Bud Talbott was the bird watcher; he was the fisherman—he really knew the wilderness. John didn't, John was a city guy and he, I think, was more comfortable in cities. And that's why I think on the camping trips he was a little more cautious, because he was more of the city guy.

While in the wilderness, as I said, he clearly enjoyed being with young people and having a chance to have extended conversation, he also never left the city. For instance, I remember John thinking of some way of creating a miniature mobile cello that he could bring on the camping trips and he spent a lot of time talking about it. And I remember one long pull of hiking in the mountains when we were talking about this all the way up. He loved to talk going up a mountain. I thought it showed an enormous amount of stamina, because that's pretty tough sometimes. He would always drop back and pick up someone and start talking. So some of the most interesting conversations would be on very tough pulls going up long mountainsides, and he was just great in those circumstances, just great, because the conversation would get so involved you would forget just how tired you were. Once we were talking about Glenn Gould [a Canadian pianist], humming and making music, and John began to make cello sounds. John was not a good singer or a musician in a pure sense, but, boy, he sure could make a good cello sound. It came out of the deepest part of his body. He sat there and leaned up against the tree and played an imaginary cello—making wonderful cello sounds. And so he would do these things, these kind-of-a-little-bit wacky things sometimes, and just enjoy it, and then he picked up his imaginary cello and off he went hiking.

Bud would be a little more cavalier about what we needed to do or not do and John was a little more concerned that nobody get hurt and let's make sure we err on the side of caution, which is not his normal personality, yet I think he was a foil. Because he sometimes felt Bud might be a little too risky, John, being a city guy, became a little more risk averse; however, there would be other times when, all of a sudden, John would flip and do something you wouldn't expect.

Pat: Can you give me an example?

Berrien: We were coming back from a pretty tough hike. I think we were in the Bear Tooth mountains in Montana. And the Bear Tooth is named because the mountains are very toothy. They go up and down sharply and it's tough hiking and we had gone up fishing for golden trout at a pretty high altitude. It had been a long day and in coming back down we almost got lost. We were coming down and we turned down too quickly, which would have taken us, shall we say, on the other side of a very steep canyon . . . so we had kind of a close call; not dangerous, but it could have been a bit of a problem had we not realized our mistake. Finally we realized we were all okay and relieved. We were coming down the mountain and all of a sudden someone saw that there was some quail or a partridge. About five or six of the game birds were down the hillside from us and John begins to say something like, "Fresh meat, fresh meat," and he picks up some rocks. Well then, all of us pick up rocks and we go running down this hillside like stone-age people throwing rocks at the partridges. John clobbers a couple of them, so we end up back in camp that night with these birds, and then John becomes very nostalgic. "Oh, I can't believe we did this!" Yet he was the guy who led it off. So here was this rather cautious person who turned, with the rest of us, down at the wrong place, and he was a little frustrated that

Bud had almost taken us down the wrong hillside and then all of a sudden the switch gets thrown and he becomes this stone-age man throwing rocks at birds.

The outfitter we used brought up another group of people and they camped with us that evening and they unveiled the fact that they bought steaks, and we never had anything like that. So all of sudden there were these steaks and we had these birds that we killed. I remember we hid them in the edge of the stream. And then John became rather resentful that all these steaks got in, "We can't have food come in on horses; we don't do that."

As I have said, John wasn't the world's greatest outdoorsman in terms of being a bird watcher or a great fisherman or anything like that, but when he would, say, catch a fish—which he might initially go into a bit reluctantly—no one enjoyed the act more than he did. It became something to be enthusiastic about, excited about, to look at, and a whole new set of things would come in: What is the best way to clean a fish? All of a sudden John would just begin to bubble over with new ideas about this: Why do they do it that way?

Pat: Did those camping trips have a particular influence on your decision to become an earth scientist?

Berrien: I was trained as a mathematician. I did my PhD in mathematics and around 1974 to 1975 I began to want to do something else. I remember one trip when I was going through my biggest angst about it. And I was talking about it, making a big deal about it, and John just looked me square in the eye and said, "Look, I have heard enough about this, clearly you have already made up your mind, just do it. Stop talking about it, just do it." And he really had, as you know, an ability, on occasion when he really wanted to use it, to pull out a knife and slice the problem right to its core. And it could be uncomfortable; it could be quite deadly. I remember feeling hurt, because I wanted to talk about it some more—about the great angst that I was going through. But in reality he was spot on that I had already decided and that I was just making a big deal about it to somehow justify it to myself when I had already decided. Flying out after the trip I remember thinking, "I have to remember that. There is a time to move on." John liked to talk about things and argue about things and so forth, yet there is a time to say "okay, all that is good, but let's go onto something else."

Pat: Did John ever talk to you about his work as a teacher?

Berrien: I think John fundamentally questioned higher education and whether or not we were doing anything right. I think he saw that when you have so many ill-prepared students entering college from college-track programs and that colleges are one of the creators of tracks and that the "getting into the college" game really governs a lot of things downstream or upstream, then something is fundamentally wrong with the system. And that is one of the things that is screwed up—elementary and high school education, which are feeding the colleges. He had a very good point and I think a lot of us in the university business wonder if we are really executing that business. This certainly is true now.

Pat: Did you ever discuss math or science education with John?

Berrien: Oh, yes. In fact he was far more knowledgeable than I, but we were both quite critical about the way that was done, including the so-called math revolution, where all of a sudden we were going to start teaching theoretical math and all we did was make a bad situation even worse. I remember saying and expressing to John that we dragged out mathematics over such a long period of time that we make it boring and hence difficult as opposed to doing it faster and making it easier. I said, "John why in the world does the average high school in America teach trigonometry in the twelfth grade while we teach geometry in the ninth grade, when you can probably teach all of it to fifth graders? What is rocket science about the ratio of the length of one side of a triangle divided by the length of the other side? John said, "You are absolutely right," and then he went just nuts. "Well; we teach addition in the first grade, subtraction in the second grade, multiplication in the third, and so forth, long division in the fifth and sixth grade. We don't teach mathematics; we drag mathematics about until everyone is put to sleep."

I remember later when he got interested in music he said, "You know to drill all these multiplication tables is like taking a piece of Bach and trying to reduce it back to scales, and you just play the scales over and over and over and you don't play music, and therefore it becomes pretty boring." We drifted on to this one day and he said, "That's why I like to play complicated pieces; I don't want to play just certain easy passages." It's so much more fun than playing nursery rhymes or something, and that's why I think he wanted to take on the great pieces of music and play them regardless if he could play them or not. Just for the life experience of doing it. So when we talked about his thinking in education, a lot of it was that we just dragged it out and we just turned it into drudgery, and then we drag out the drudgery. It's as if we almost went about it to bore people.

He was spot on and later when I thought about it, I felt it's just stupid the way I remember being taught in grammar school. He really saw the system very clearly, but it's extremely difficult to change the system. That was another thing I think John was very frustrated by.

Pat: Holt's contrarian thinking could sometimes lead him to take actions that, by most people's thinking, would be considered eccentric.

Berrien: There were these beliefs that he had. For instance, John picked me up at an airport en route to a camping trip, and we had a three-hour drive to connect with everyone else. That day, John had pretty bad hay fever or allergy. So he began almost immediately to tell me about this new hay fever theory—you get rid of the hay fever if you let all of your sinuses just drain. And therefore you shouldn't blow your nose, you shouldn't sneeze, you shouldn't use a handkerchief and it was the damnedest thing I had ever seen in my life. I said "John, this is nuts!" He said, "Oh no, no. Handkerchiefs are the act of the devil" or something. We had this three-hour debate about where handkerchiefs came from. And it was just something that he had got in his mind that day and he wasn't going to take any antihistamines and he wasn't going to use a handkerchief—he was just going to let his nose run. And so he had this theory, which arose from his questioning of the norm. I think this was very revealing. This is exactly what he did all of his life. Take something that is common; this is the way you did something, and John would turn it on its head and say, "Maybe not." I am not altogether convinced that blowing your nose until your ears pop is a good idea either. He was always interested in questioning something. And it was remarkable what he would come up with to question.

Pat: When you knew John in the 1970s it was at a point when he was giving up on the school reform movement and he hadn't quite come around to homeschooling, so you knew him at this time when he was asking a lot of questions and probing and trying to find out about it.

Berrien: What's interesting to me is that there were two aspects of homeschooling that I remember very distinctly that we talked about. One was that he foresaw the enormous success that homeschooling could achieve and has achieved. He also saw very clearly and had some deep concerns about the potential rise in religious fundamentalism that could flourish in a purely homeschooling environment where you are not challenged by, say, scientific facts. He knew it could become a doctrinaire element and he was quite conflicted about that and didn't know just what should be done. Because the last thing John would go for would be to put some regulation on homeschooling. He would really pound you if you said something like that.

I remember that we were on one long hike in the rain, and I remember him arguing with himself—in a way that I do not remember him doing all that often. I remember this distinctly that he was almost playing chess with himself as to how to work this out. Later, we were hanging out in Pinedale, Wyoming for a day before heading to the airplane, and I was asking him about it, and he was saying that it was really still bothering him that he had been thinking about this for a long time, and he then went into some of the nuances. He painted a very clear picture of the ups and the downs—with even more detail than I normally had heard from John. He saw the great potential of homeschooling, but he was also very worried about it, and some of his concerns you see now. There are a lot of fundamentalist areas, particularly in the United States, where there is wonderful homeschooling being done, and yet the concept of evolution doesn't get taught. The earth was created 5437 years ago. Some really nutty stuff and that is, as John saw, a real "downside."

Pat: Though John was involved a lot in political activism early and into in his midlife, I think his perspective on how to create meaningful social change altered as he got older.

Berrien: At that stage in life he really wasn't interested in politics. I mean it wasn't something that he was passionate about anymore. He was always much more interested in what individuals could do.

Pat: Would you say that John had an influence on you and what would that be if he did?

Berrien: Oh, goodness gracious yes, yes. The main thing was try to see things clearly and act on what you really thought was important.

Also, I think there were some things that I think he did later in his life that caused me also to be careful. I think the one thing that bothered Strobe and me, but Strobe in some ways the most because he saw it earlier, and that was when John developed cancer. John refused conventional medicine thinking, "No I am going to cure it, I am going to master it."

He ran the risk of viewing the world differently and then have that bite you. This was sad.

Dr. Berrien Moore III is an internationally recognized Earth scientist who has been honored by the National Aeronautics and Space Administration (NASA) and the National Oceanic and Atmospheric Administration (NOAA). He is Vice President of Weather & Climate Programs and Dean at the College of Atmospheric & Geographic Science at the University of Oklahoma, and Director of the National Weather Center.

Cracker-Barrel Writing

By Thomas Armstrong

When I was in my early twenties (I'm 62 now), John Holt was sort of like a rock star to me. His book *How Children Fail* (1964/1982) was the crème de la crème of a whole cornucopia of education books that came out in the 1960s, including George Dennison's (1969) *Lives of Children*, Herb Kohl's (1967) *36 Children*, Jonathan Kozol's (1967) *Death at an Early Age*, and James Herndon's (1965) *The Way It Spozed To Be*. I treasured all of those books, but John Holt's book seemed to ring truest; he seemed to speak with the clearest voice about respecting the needs of children in the classroom. Only Maria Montessori, in my mind, occupied a similar pinnacle of awe and adulation among all the figures in education at that time who wrote about children and learning (and I'm not sure if I have even changed that estimation in the forty years that have elapsed since I first read them).

That's why I felt so fortunate to meet John Holt three times throughout the 1970s and 1980s, each time at a different stage of my teaching career. The first time I met him was in 1975, while I was doing my student teaching through the University of Massachusetts School of Education, at the Cambridge Alternative Public School (CAPS) in Cambridge, Massachusetts (now known as the Graham and Parks Alternative Public School). I'm not sure now what the specific motivation was, but I contacted Holt Associates and was surprised and delighted when John Holt offered to meet with us (myself and a small group of fifth grade students) at his office in Boston. I remember how John lay on the floor with his elbow on the carpet and his feet extending sideways, as he spoke with us. This informal attitude seemed to put everyone at ease, and suggested to me that John was willing to "come down" to the level of the students as a way of making better contact with them. The other thing that I distinctly remember about the meeting is what happened between him and a particular student of mine. CAPS was an interesting school with a mixture of children from well-educated, high socio-economic, highly motivated families (Matt Damon and Ben Affleck would become students there only two or three years after I left), and students from low-income projects in Cambridge.

One of the students I brought to the meeting was an African-American girl from the projects. I had been having a great deal of difficulty with her in the course of my student teaching. She was frequently noncompliant and abusive, thinking nothing of punching me in the gut if she got angry (we had a bit more latitude in tolerating behaviors in those alternative school days). In retrospect, I'm amazed that I actually brought her to the meeting given her negative behaviors (perhaps I had arranged it as an incentive to get her to behave more appropriately?). But what surprised me was that in the presence of John Holt she almost melted. She became sweet, kind, and curious. I can still picture her bright shining face and feel her soft guileless affect as she asked John several good questions and listened to the responses attentively. This helped to wake me up to the fact that when you treat children with respect (as Holt did in his office with my students), then children will respect you and feel freer to express what is inside of them.

The second time I met John Holt was only a year or two later, when I was engaged in my first full-time teaching job as a learning disability specialist with the Montreal Catholic School Commission (in 1976–1977, all schools in Montreal, Canada were either Catholic or Protestant; I understand that this practice was abolished in 1998 and secular institutions have since replaced them). There was a group in Montreal called the Society for Emotionally Disturbed Children and they, in conjunction with some other education groups, put on a special education conference that was really one of the best conferences I've ever attended. They had an all-star line-up of speakers, from the maverick educator George von Hilsheimer (1970) (who at the time was also a special hero of mine because of the eclectic and holistic nature of his book *How to Live with Your Special Child*) to the special education pioneer William Cruickshank, who I remember said at the conference that he and Samuel J. Kirk had "invented" the concept of learning disabilities in a Chicago hotel room in 1962! John Holt was also a speaker at the conference, and I admit that I tailed him like a groupie. He walked around with a backpack on, which wasn't something that people commonly did at that time, so it struck me as a bit eccentric; although now, of course, everyone does it (a man ahead of his time). Nevertheless, I pestered him with questions, which he patiently answered. During his talk, I remember him asking the audience if anyone knew about any research linking standardized testing with anxiety. He'd already written about this in *How Children Fail* (1964/1982), but it really struck me when he said it at the conference, that there should be this link between the psychological/physiological state of anxiety and the use of those wicked tests. I was studying psychosynthesis at the time (a positive psychology developed by an Italian psychiatrist and disciple of Freud named Roberto Assagioli), and was very interested in making these kinds of links between psychological states and educational environments.

One of the key events at the conference was a debate between John Holt and William Cruikshank. In addition to "inventing learning disabilities," Cruikshank was known for creating the "Cruikshank classroom"—a special education classroom that was stimulus-free (no pictures on the walls, learning materials put away in cupboards, a bare study carrel, etc.). It was believed (wrongly, we know now) that the "hyperkinetic child" (a term then used to describe what we currently call ADHD), would be catapulted into hyperactive behavior if there was too much stimulation around him. The female teacher was even advised not to wear red lipstick, as Cruikshank and his colleagues believed it would trigger a hyperactive response! Anyway, I was really looking forward to this debate between a straight-laced academic figure and a leader of the open education movement. The debate turned out to be horrible. It represented a good example of people talking in different paradigms. They were so far apart on so many issues that they just talked past each other, and eventually the whole affair turned into the intellectual equivalent of a freestyle mud wrestling contest. I was disappointed because I was hoping to see John achieve a knockout punch. Instead, he seemed a bit cowed and confused by Cruikshank's intellectual arrogance, and I can't say as I blamed him.

The third and last time that I had the opportunity to meet John was in 1980 when I was teaching in special education at the Mt. Diablo Unified School District in northern California. John was speaking at an event held at Stern Grove, a lovely park in the middle of San Francisco, which in addition to hosting talks like John's, also held an annual free music festival every summer. I remember John brought his cello to the event. He had just written his book *Never Too Late: My Musical Life Story* (1978/1991), which gives an account of his taking up the cello at the age of 40. One thing that amazed me was that during breaks he allowed people, including children, to practice playing his cello. He didn't even hover around them worrying that they might damage it (which is what *I'd* be doing!). Again, there was this element of deep trust in people (especially children) that seemed to mark his personality. One thing I do remember is that while he was talking in the indoor facility at Stern Grove, there were a number of children crying and talking, and John seemed irritated by this, and finally he stopped and said to the parents that if they couldn't keep their kids quiet they should remove them from the premises. I recall that this incident put a bit of a damper on the image I had of John as an eternally beneficent figure toward children. Of course, I should have known all along that there was this element of sometimes brutal honesty in John that didn't mince words. Holt did, after all, write in *How Children Fail* (1964/1982)

> If a child asks me to do something that I don't want to do, I tell him that I won't do it because I don't want to do it, instead of giving him a list of "good" reasons sounding as if they had come down from the Supreme Court. (p. 283)

At any rate, I remember leaving Stern Grove feeling a little less hero worship for John, which, of course, is as it should be.

Although I never saw John again, I did have contact with him through correspondence over the next two or three years. After I quit teaching in 1981, I put my energies into working on a book that lambasted the whole notion of "learning disabilities." At the time, the book was called *The Learning Disability Lie*. I wrote to John about my project, and he wrote back that he didn't think the title was such a good one because he didn't believe that educators were intentionally "lying" about learning disabilities, only that they had the wrong concepts. As a result of this, I re-titled the book *The Learning Disability Trap* (it later came out as *In Their Own Way: Discovering and Encouraging Your Child's Personal Learning Style* (2000)). I sent a copy of the material I had written thus far (perhaps two or three chapters) to John, and received a long letter from him in return giving me advice on how to improve the manuscript. One of the pieces of feedback that I received from him was that my writing was too intellectual, too bookish, too much of the university, and not conversational enough. He told me to write as if I was sitting across the cracker barrel from someone telling a story. I've tried to remember that advice ever since.

In preparation for this chapter, I re-read *How Children Fail* (1964/1982), and rediscovered that cracker-barrel style of writing echoing throughout the book. It amazed me to think that many sections of the book were written in the 1950s, in the midst of an America caught up in conventional, conformist, straitjacket thinking about matters related to education. This was the age of *Why Johnny Can't Read* (1955) (he needs phonics), segregated schools, and the Iowa Test of Basic Skills. Of course, the book didn't come out until 1964, when the plastic culture of the 1950s was beginning to melt into the 1960s counter-cultural scene, but still his book should be considered revolutionary given the times in which they were written. In re-reading the book, I felt once again those clear cadences, those child-centered passages that felt like a burst of fresh air rushing into a congested room. One passage that particularly stirs me is the following:

> We adults destroy most of the intellectual and creative capacity of children by the things we do to them or make

them do. We destroy this capacity above all by making them afraid, afraid of not doing what other people want, of not pleasing, of making mistakes, of failing, of being *wrong*. Thus we make them afraid to gamble, afraid to experiment, afraid to try the difficult and the unknown. (Holt, 1964/1982, p. 274)

Of course, there are many other things about John Holt's work that I've left out of this brief account: his specific prescriptions for re-visioning teaching and learning, his recommendations for school reform, and most especially his work as a pioneer of the homeschooling (or unschooling) movement. However, I'm focused here with what I feel to be his fundamental message: that we need to respect the child just as we respect any human being. I think if John were alive today, he would be a champion of the rights of minorities, women, the disabled, people in the LGBTQ community, and other oppressed people. But he would also be ahead of the rest in pushing for the rights of children (as he did in his radical and largely misunderstood book, *Escape from Childhood* (1974/2013)). Today, in many parts of the world, these rights simply don't exist (note, for example, the use of children as soldiers, sweatshop workers, and sex slaves around the world). And even in our so-called enlightened society, we are still oppressing children through our educational practices (mandatory standardized testing, a rigid national curriculum, a corporatized classroom, etc.), and through the physical, sexual, and psychological abuse that takes place every day in homes and communities across the nation. John would be waving the flag of liberty for those children. Let's take up the flag and fight for the rights of all children everywhere. I think John would be happy about that.

References

Armstrong, T. (2000). *In Their Own Way: Discovering and Encouraging Your Child's Personal Learning Style* (revised). New York, NY: Jeremy P. Tarcher/Putnam.

Dennison, G. (1970). *Lives of children: The story of the first street school.* New York, NY: Vintage Books. (Original work published 1969)

Flesch, R. (1985). *Why Johnny Can't Read: And what you can do about it.* New York, NY: Harper & Row. (Original work published 1955)

Herndon, J. (1968). *The way it spozed to be: A report on the classroom war behind the crisis of our schools.* New York, NY: Simon and Schuster. (Original work published 1965)

Hilsheimer, G. V. (1970). *How to Live with Your Special Child.* Acropolis Books.

Holt, J. (2013). *Escape from childhood: The needs and rights of children.* Medford, MA: HoltGWS LLC. (Original work published 1974)

Holt, J. (1991). *Never too late: My musical life story.* USA: Da Capo Press. (Original work published 1978)

Holt, J. (1982). *How children fail* (Revised ed.). USA: Da Capo Press. (Original work published 1964)

Kohl, H. (1988). *36 children.* New York, NY: Plume. (Original work published 1967)

Kozol, J. (1970). *Death at an early age.* New York, NY: Bantam Books. (Original work published 1967)

Thomas Armstrong, PhD is an author and speaker with over one million copies of his books in print on issues related to learning and human development. He is the author of fifteen books, translated into 26 languages, including: Multiple Intelligences in the Classroom; In Their Own Way; Awakening Your Child's Natural Genius; 7 Kinds of Smart; The Myth of the A.*D.D. Child*; and *Neurodiversity in the Classroom: Strength-Based Strategies to Help Students with Special Needs Achieve Success in School and Life.* He lives in Sonoma County, California with his wife Barbara Turner, PhD, a sandplay psychotherapist, and two Shih Tzu dogs. He can be reached at: thomas@thomasarmstrong. Information about his work is available at: www.thomasarmstrong.com.

Learner-Centered Schools

By Jerry Mintz

I first met John Holt at Goddard College in the mid-1960s. I had read some of his work and was interested in finding a school to teach where these ideas were being practiced. John took contact information from me and, surprisingly, he kept in touch.

Meanwhile I didn't find a school to teach in. Instead I began to pursue the idea of starting my own school using these concepts. I had interned at a school in upstate New York that was based on Summerhill School in England. A.S. Neill had started Summerhill, and it was based on trusting children with freedom and using a democratic decision-making process.

Not long after I opened my school I got a note from John asking me if I had found a school in which to teach. I wrote back to him and told him that I hadn't and therefore had started my own school. He immediately put our school on his list of recommended schools. This gave us crucial support, particularly staff members who were interested in a learner-centered philosophy. It also helped with fundraising to have John's support.

In the next several years I visited John whenever I went to Boston. Over the years his philosophy shifted to the point that he began to believe that schools were not viable institutions that would encourage a learner-centered approach. Eventually, after writing *Teach Your Own*, (1981/2003) he simply suggested that people abandon schools and start home educating. I remember discussing this with him in his office. He couldn't believe that children would willingly go to any school if they didn't have to go to school. I told him that at our school students didn't have to go to classes if they didn't want to and could ask for any classes they wanted. And they could just hang out with friends at the school, play games or organize trips if they wanted. Our school was based on the belief that children are natural learners and if you support a good learning environment, they will want to be there. In fact, since the school ran democratically, the students passed a rule that the school should *never* close for snow days, and this should be announced on the radio.

They even tried to vote out the summer vacation, which worked until the teachers said they needed a break!

In 1984 we were able to sponsor a talk by John to come to Vermont. Through that talk, at the city auditorium, the first state organization of homeschoolers and alternative schools was created. That became the Vermont Homeschooler's Association. John stayed overnight at the emergency shelter we were running and I remember that we gave him the best room in the place, but it was also the director's room where the phone would ring. We got a call from a kid that night who had run away from the shelter but now was calling us to talk about coming back. We talked to him and tried to take the phone out of the room. But John said, "No, no, I want to hear this conversation!" So he listened to us talk the kid back to the shelter. I think that it was a really interesting experience for John. At the same time we had a meeting of the homeschoolers at the boarding part of our school.

Subsequently John did agree that it was possible to have a school that students did want to go to. Our approach was very similar to what is called unschooling today.

References

Holt, J., & Farenga, P. (2003). *Teach your own: The John Holt book of homeschooling* (Revised ed.). USA: Da Capo Press. (Original work published 1981.)

Jerry Mintz has been a leading voice in the alternative school movement for over thirty years. He was a public school teacher and principal, and, for seventeen years, an independent alternative school principal. In 1989, he founded the Alternative Education Resource Organization and has helped found over 50 alternative schools and organizations. He has been on National Public Radio, the major TV networks, in *The New York Times*, *Newsday*, and many other publications. He was Editor-in-Chief for the *Handbook of Alternative Education*, and the *Almanac of Education Choices*. He is the author of *No Homework and Recess All Day: How to Have Freedom and Democracy in Education*. Co-editor of *Turning Points: 35 Visionaries in Education Tell Their Own Stories*. He appeared in a recent TEDx talk. He continues to lecture and consult around the world.

A Close Family Friend
By Peggy Hughes

In 1958, while John Holt was teaching the fifth-grade class at Shady Hill he describes in *How Children Fail* (1964/1982), he fell into the habit of walking home from school past our house on Sparks Street in Cambridge so we could talk about his day over a cup of tea. My daughter Sarah was in that class, and I will never forget the powerful effect his ideas had on me.

After the success of that first book, the sales of his many later books influenced generations of other families, but in our family he always filled a special non-academic role. Sarah had him in class, her younger sister Kathy knew him as a friend in our kitchen, and Bill, the youngest, whose passionate personality and struggles with the cello John (1978/1991) described in *Never Too Late,* knew him as a beginning musician.

That determined 9-year-old cellist went with us on Fridays to sit in long waiting lines on the floor of Symphony Hall in Boston to get rush seat tickets for the regular afternoon concert. We ate picnic lunches, read the paper, knitted, played chess. One autumn day, the new headmaster at Shady Hill decreed Friday afternoons to be for football practice. Nine-year-old boys playing contact football? John fortified my opposition to an edict that I would never have dared mount on my own. It was the old fight: Who owns the child, parent or school? Thanks to John's backing we continued to go to Symphony Hall those Friday afternoons, and my children went to another school the next year.

Some years later we moved to Denmark and John came to stay, often for long visits. I was teaching in one of the so-called "Little" Schools that had been founded at the end of the Second World War by Danish parents, many of them past members of the Resistance Movement, who wanted to create a better society. John knew like-minded educators in Sweden and Denmark and came often to stay with us to talk about kids with people who thought alike. I had visited the Bagsværd Ny Lilleskole at the end of our first year in Denmark and asked the head teacher for a job. John loved spending time in my school.

Back in John's Boston office during one summer I suggested filming the goings-on in the school's old factory building. He loved the idea. Fred Wiseman's recent hair-raising *High School* (1968) documentary showed just how awful a conventional school can be. With shameless lack of modesty I thought I'd like to it try my hand at filming another kind of educational environment. I still marvel that John agreed to invest in the heavy 16mm Beaulieu and the complicated sound equipment that went with it. He did however, and back in Denmark, I began to carry the camera around every day as I peered into whatever was going on. A dark Scandinavian winter presented serious light limitations, and sound recording was even more demanding than the camera. Naturally the kids were intrigued by the equipment and loved learning how to operate it. They proved invaluable with the sound, which had to be edited and synched later. Viewed from today's digital luxuries, that cumbersome equipment was not easy for us rank beginners.

The school building was an unprepossessing concrete shell of a space that at the start of every school year the kids divided up with stacks of wooden Tuborg beer cases. Partition walls were five or six boxes high arranged rather like the cubicles in today's corporate spaces. Looking down the length of the room from the entrance, you could see movement everywhere. A lot of people were involved in their various interests; some quiet, some not so. Visible were a dozen or so rooms in which it was possible for discussions to take place that were inaudible in the neighboring spaces. One hundred or so adults and kids were following up their own interests, reading, talking, doing woodwork, and playing games. John spoke no Danish but during his many visits to the school he watched everything closely and particularly loved the music and gymnastics. The general body language confirmed so much that he was thinking, and all the teachers spoke good English for his questions and comments.

The amateurish film that resulted was *We Have to Call It School* (1974). It did prove an asset to his lectures later when audiences wanted to know what his ideas would look like if put into practice. The place certainly looked nothing like a place to which most American parents would imagine sending a child. And indeed many Danish parents of school-age children were just as doubtful. Government funding for a school like this was unique to Denmark then. Any ten parents who wanted to make a learning environment where desks were not in rows, could get the necessary educational financing. The after-war years when the country was decidedly left leaning made the policy workable among liberal Danes, and John found it a perfect lab example of some of his own theories. Waiting until a child wants to learn to read makes it feasible to teach him or her in thirty hours of one-on-one teaching. The film shows that happening. To encourage confidence, give a boy skill in operating a dangerous tool. One of the teachers, a steel worker before being a teacher, supplied the equipment and welders' masks to interested boys. A twelve-year-old then made the steel frame for a bike trailer. The glee of those kids wearing welders' masks with sparks flying around their heads was a sight to see.

The energetic atmosphere was cultivated by the teachers, each of whom arrived daily full of a zest that felt like the creative force of other kinds of intentional communities where the instigators are fired up by knowing they are onto something important.

My husband and I found living in Denmark to be an awakening from the rigidity and horror of the Nixon years at home and an escape to a haven of adjusted people living rational, worry-free lives. Never mind that the winters were dark and rainy and seemed to last without end; we wanted to stay forever.

John's delight in Danish society matched ours. He even asked me to look into the possibility of his moving there, too. He loved the competence of little kids in public life. I remember his pleasure one day watching a seven-year-old standing at the top of a department store escalator beside a baby brother in a stroller, waiting for Mum. Every shopper getting off the escalator stopped to greet him. John later talked about him and the polite adults who spoke to him in *Escape From Childhood: The Needs and Rights of Children* (1974/2013).

Today's Denmark is not quite as idyllic as we found it to be then, but John's perceptions of it as a guest were solid confirmations of our own gut feelings. I still think that Danish society in the sixties and seventies put together some of mankind's best ideas and that its brand of socialism produced liberal and practical ways of raising children. In my view the present country remains a place to emulate for the rest of Europe.

A different child-related consequence of the Danish war years was the development of a new variety of government-sponsored playgrounds. During the German occupation, kids played spontaneously in vacant lots and created games out of anything at hand. They loved junk of all kinds, and collected it from collapsing buildings, industrial wastes of various sorts, leftover pipes, ropes, and junk. They created worlds of their own from things that grown-ups had thrown away. Out of this odd resource evolved Adventure Playgounds. Of course they were a terrible sight to passers-by, so municipal governments surrounded them with high fences and then arranged for watchers with some childcare qualifications, a bit like camp counselors, to oversee them and authenticate activities. Many were in mid-city locations, some were in suburbia, and within all of them the players had permission to do anything within life-threatening safety limits. Stretched between two neighboring buildings one had a long rope with an attached homemade funicular car that travelled its length. Passengers screamed with joy. Piles of used and discarded lumber or remnants from lumberyards, boxes of all kinds, plastic and canvas sheeting were collected. They built small sheds to act as clubhouses, and after their original novelty wore off, a popular activity might be to destroy them, even occasionally by fire. Arson on a small scale can be wildly exciting and satisfying, especially if condoned by the watchers present.

The idea for these playgrounds travelled to London where the Blitz provided unlimited resources. City planners noted an interesting development; wherever these playgrounds appeared, vandalism in the nearby neighborhood ceased. Most inner-city destruction is found in and around school buildings, since hatred for school is nearly universal. Around the Adventure Playgrounds there are almost no broken windows.

John found these kid-created places to be strong confirmations of his philosophy, and after we all regretfully returned to the United States from Denmark, he asked me to look into setting up such a playground near the Boston harbor docks. It was an illuminating experience for me in City Hall urban planning. We found a nearby low-income housing project that would supply plenty of kids, and the parents we visited thought it was a great idea, but the concept never took off. Even after some ideal space became available near the project beside the huge container loading docks, junk as childhood enrichment was not an idea that sold in Boston.

John's office during the time of this effort was as Danish as we could make it. We furnished it with Ikea furniture, including a long, low table where we all ate our communal lunch. This was an inviolable custom in Copenhagen offices as well as in our school. John's desk, entirely surrounded by his unique filing system in piles on the floor, was at one end of the main room. In the middle were five or six chairs so we could all sit down and talk while we ate. In time two lawyers, whose office was just down the hall, joined us every day. We had heated conversations, lots of laughs, a great deal of political talk and planning for John's increasingly busy lecture and book-signing trips.

A favorite memory from then is of his whiz-of-a-secretary, Lynn Schultz, a beauty who typed like the wind. John had invited her to the upstairs dining room at the Ritz for her birthday lunch. At the appointed time, Lynn appeared at the entrance of the restaurant dressed for a formal meal. The pompous headwaiter refused to admit her saying her skirt was too short. You will know exactly what John's reaction was. He exploded, said he would never use the restaurant again—and he never did. When he died, Lynn wrote to me, "He taught me two important things. How to pick a ripe melon, and how to take no shit."

Some years later, our family moved to a small town in Maine where we had a farm. John was there frequently with us, taking part in everything. He shoveled seaweed from the beach for the compost pile, helped in the cow barn. One day I was working in a beehive and he was watching. After I told him that the bees were completely harmless, much too busy with their work to bother a spectator, one promptly zoomed in and stung his bald head. He roared with laugher and said he'd never again believe a thing I said.

He played his cello for long hours on the farmhouse porch with Penobscot Bay behind him, and made our dinners hilarious when he recited long Stanley Holloway verses. Today I keep a picture of him over my desk sitting on the porch wearing his pork pie hat, his mouth full of food, exploding with laughter, and a hand on the head of an Irish wolfhound who has just eaten his sandwich. It breaks me up to look at it.

He was the closest friend of my long life. I have just celebrated my 91st birthday and I miss him as much now as the year he died. Shared habits of thought, a joke he would have relished, maddening news on the political scene bring him to mind every day.

References

Holt, J. (1991). *Never too late: My musical life story*. USA: Da Capo Press. (Original work published 1978)
Holt, J. (1982). *How children fail* (Revised ed.). USA: Da Capo Press. (Original work published 1964)
Holt, J., (Producer), & Hughes, P. (Director). (1974). *We have to call it school*. USA: Holt Associates.
Wiseman, F. (Producer), & (Director). (1968). *High School*. USA: OSTI Productions.

Peggy Hughes's life included working for the Army Medical Corps during WWII, then marrying and raising three children in Cambridge MA. Moving to Maine as a dairy farmer, she and her family escaped the Nixon years in the United States and spent four years in Denmark where she taught in a free school. The Danish example of factory-built housing inspired her to travel to Russia during the early Perestroika years where she was a principal in three unsuccessful Joint Ventures. Defeated there, she brought the technology to the United States and ran an import business that built 46 Danish-manufactured houses in the U.S., from Wisconsin to New England. She now lives in Northampton, MA where she gardens extensively and studies French, travelling often to France where she continues her lifelong passion, watercolor painting.

What Else Do You See?

By Merloyd Lawrence

A few months before his death, when his cancer had returned, John wrote:

> I am facing a personal danger which is rather like the danger we all face from nuclear war, which might carry us all away. Meanwhile—I don't agree with people like Lifton who call it a psychic numbing—we live and work as best we can, and get some fun out of life as we do it. That will be my plan. (J. Holt, personal communication, May 6, 1985)

This voice and example lives on with all of us who knew him. He managed at the end, as he had all his life, to live entirely in the present. Everything around him, whether trees in the Public Garden, well-made scrambled eggs, and of course small children, deserved intense observation and enjoyment. When he would come over to our house for "high tea," each bite of Linzer torte could well have been the first bite ever taken in history.

John once wrote about one of his heroes, the Swiss scientist Louis Agassiz, who began a college course by placing a single fish on a plate and asking his students to describe it. Every time they brought him their papers thinking that they had said all there was to say, he asked, "What else?" He did not stop until they had seen and recorded a hundred times more than at first try. John might well have been describing himself when he went on to write, "It is this ability to see, and then to describe accurately what was seen, that is the hallmark of the great naturalist" (Holt, 1989, p. 133).

The same ability made John's books, from *How Children Fail* (1964/1982) to the posthumous *Learning All the Time* (1989), live on in millions of copies and dozens of languages around the world. To read John's work is to see children for the first time.

John's enduring legacy took on some more curious turns. After learning that his editor was going to get married, he arrived one day with his wedding present. In a lumpy plastic bag that appeared to be full of nothing but dirt, was a tangle of worms. John had been experimenting with composting and even "how to grow protein in the city" and was not inclined to leave this to experts in the Department of Agriculture; he had been nurturing a crop of small pink worms in his Beacon Hill apartment. These he fed by borrowing a wheelbarrow from the hardware store and gathering leaves in the park. Later experiments proved that old newspapers would also do nicely. Today, twenty-seven years later, the descendants of his wedding present thrive in our city compost heap.

"One of the great tasks of our life is to find our best work, work worth doing for its own sake." This was one of the little homemade or found proverbs that John would send his friends. He discovered that work early on. As a writer who, in George Dennison's words, always wanted "to make the world a better place," he found his best work. I was lucky to be able to join him in that work, as his editor, partway through, when he revised *How Children Fail* (1982a) and *How Children Learn* (1983) into the much longer versions that now live on. He knew just what he wanted to write and brought a simplicity and modesty to the work that I've never seen in a writer before.

Each new book began with a short, to-the-point letter that stated what he wanted to do, quite unlike the usual inflated proposals from authors and agents in that he would do exactly what he said he would do. While he was open to a bit of polishing here and there, he actually knew just what made good writing and I learned more than I could offer.

Everything that John put into words in books, letters, or talks, was first hand. Whether he was describing didactic adults or children at play, or even a head cold, his intent was to make sense of his experience. His avoidance of theory brought an unusual modesty. He brushed off the success of his best selling titles as "mostly an accident." In the 1970s the great demand from colleges and organizations for him to lecture did not go to his head. John said, "I thought I was 'changing people' but discovered that when I was introduced as 'a controversial speaker' that was code for 'this guy is full of shit, pay no attention.'"

The roots of both this modesty and John's acute observations ran deep. "Every branch of science rests on assumptions," he once wrote (1982b). The mission of questioning those assumptions, whether in views about "slow" children, in notions that adults could not learn music well (challenged in his lovely memoir (1978/1991)) or in his calm, logical, and always kindly correspondence with others of fixed opinions—educators, scientists, creationists or politicians—lives on for all of us in his writing and in his example.

References

Holt, J. (1991). *Never too late: My musical life story*. USA: Da Capo Press. (Original work published 1978)

Holt, J. (1989). *Learning all the time: How small children begin to read, write, count, and investigate the world, without being taught*. USA: Da Capo Press.

Holt, J. (1983). *How children learn* (Revised ed.). USA: Da Capo Press. (Original work published 1967.)

Holt, J. (1982a). *How children fail* (Revised ed.). USA: Da Capo Press. (Original work published 1964)

Holt, J. (1982b). Letter to the Editor, *Boston Globe*, January 9, 1982.

Merloyd Lawrence was John's longtime editor. *Learning All the Time, Never Too Late* and the second editions of *How Children Fail* and *How Children Learn* are published under her imprint at Da Capo Press. As neighbors and close friends, they enjoyed marathon lunches and high teas and a love of Boston's Public Garden.

The Nickel and Dime Theory about Social Change

By Wendy Priesnitz

I first came across John Holt's books *How Children Fail* (1964/1982) and *How Children Learn* (1967/1983) when I was in teachers' college in 1968 to 1969, along with books by other school reformers. The ideas excited me, but the one-year course was so intense that I didn't have much time to think; I was too busy memorizing the theory and writing exams, interspersed with a few weeks of practice teaching. After I graduated and got a teaching job I quickly discovered, somewhat to my surprise, that I was spending most of my time trying to motivate children who were rebelling at the coercion and bored with the out-of-context, secondhand information. After less than one school year I, too, felt rebellious and bored, and terminated my career as a schoolteacher.

Then I did what I should have done while I was attending teachers' college: I began my self-education about how people learn by observing children. I remembered what John Holt had written about getting in the way of children's learning. Around the same time, I met and married my husband Rolf, who agreed with me that our yet-to-be-born children wouldn't go to school. A few years later, after much thinking and writing of my own, I picked up *Escape from Childhood* (1974/2013) and discovered that, as I had, John Holt had moved beyond schools. That book affirmed what I had discovered about how our culture has low expectations of and respect for children—an injustice that I hoped to circumvent as our young family explored living without school. In addition, I was encouraged that John, like me, figured this out firsthand, through observation of children rather than by reading other people's work or taking courses at the academy. Years later, when I was asked by an academic which writers had influenced my thinking about self-directed learning, I said—to his horror—that I'd figured it out for myself, because to have done otherwise would be incongruous. So I chuckled when I read John's comment in *A Life Worth Living: The Selected Letters of John Holt* (1990): "There seems to me a suggestion [. . .] that in learning about the world, other people's books are more important than observation. With this view I most emphatically and strongly disagree" (p. 55).

In order that Rolf and I could both stay at home to facilitate our young daughters' self-directed learning adventure, we launched a home-based publishing business and our first magazine, *Natural Life*, in 1976. As did many people in those early days of the modern homeschooling movement, we shared our adventure with John, mailing him some copies of the magazine and writing about our homeschooling journey. At the same time, in an attempt to connect with other homeschooling families, I also shared our family's homeschooling status on my editorial page in *Natural Life Magazine* (www.naturallifemagazine.com). Then, as a way of educating both school officials and other families about the legality of homeschooling, I launched the Canadian Alliance of Homeschoolers—the country's first support/advocacy group. Those efforts were part of a wonderful period when a small but growing number of pioneering North American homeschooling families—many of whom became homeschooling activists in their own provinces and states—came together in support and advocacy. It also led to a huge number of speaking requests for John; along with other local families, we brought him to Toronto to help spread the word about this revolutionary notion for educating children.

In early 1977, John told us about his plan to start a newsletter. He said that he found himself at the center of a growing homeschooling letter-writing network and that, since he was writing similar letters to a number of people, he thought a newsletter would be a good way to connect everyone and share ideas. He said he didn't know anything about publishing and, since he admired *Natural Life*, he asked us for advice. So, by phone, Rolf outlined the basics and gave him some suggestions.

Not long after, we received the first issue of *Growing Without Schooling* (*GWS*) in the mail. In *Natural Life's* August 1977 issue I wrote:

> We've just received a note from John Holt, author of *Escape from Childhood* and a number of other excellent books about the terrible way society and schools treat our children. He sent along the first issue of his four-page newsletter called *GWS*.
>
> It is basically about ways in which people, young or old, can learn and do things, acquire skills, and find interesting and useful work, without having to go through the process of school.

> Mostly, it promises to be about people who want to take or keep their children out of school, and about what they might do instead. It is an exchange and much of this and future issues will come from readers sharing ideas, feelings, experiences, and needs.
>
> *Natural Life* will continue to feature articles about the logistics of keeping your kids out of the public school system and schools in general. So *GWS* is a very welcome support and inspiration to those of us involved in our young children's education. (p. 16)

John kept us informed about the newsletter's development, and we published further announcements about it since it was, at the time, the only publication of its kind. *Natural Life Magazine* had both Canadian and U.S. editions, and was sold on newsstands across North America. As a result of that, and coverage in other magazines like *Mother Earth News* (www.motherearthnews.com/) *GWS* received a great deal of mail, many asking questions about homeschooling legalities. Since John and his small staff couldn't easily answer the Canadian queries, they began to regularly bundle up those letters and mail them off to me for a response. Likewise, when I received homeschooling queries from our American readers, I referred them to the *GWS* office, lessening the burden of the deluge of mail on our family's time and resources, and continuing the exchange of information and support with John and his staff.

John was, famously, a prolific letter writer. Sometimes, we'd receive a utilitarian note typed on a postcard; other times, he'd send a long and thoughtful letter about life, children, learning, self-reliance alternative economics, or pcacc (all topics we were writing about in *Natural Life*). He discussed his frustration with people who were still trying to reform schools, who felt that homeschooling is elitist, and other criticisms by progressives that persist today. He also shared with me his frustration at not having enough time to do all the writing he'd like—books, *GWS*, and letters—let alone to pursue his passion for music.

In spite of that frustration, he felt his work about education was very important in terms of correcting injustice in the world. In the first issue of *GWS*, John (1977, August) wrote that by starting the newsletter, he and his staff were "putting into practice a nickel and dime theory about social change, which is, that important and lasting social change always comes slowly, and only when people change their lives . . ." (p. 1). That resonated with me, because it was exactly what I had set out to do with our publishing business, and with my writing and advocacy. He went on to describe the incremental process of making change and his part in it, which was to help grow the minority who do not believe in compulsory schooling and who believe that children can be trusted to learn about the world "without much adult coercion or interference" (p. 1).

As my advocacy role expanded after our family had a few run-ins with arrogant school board officials and uninformed social services people, I took strength from watching the *GWS* directory of individuals and groups swell in size as the homeschooling movement grew. In general, the newsletter's format anticipated today's social media, where people can connect with others of like mind, share ideas and experiences, find inspiration and support, and commiserate when things go wrong. *GWS* also—most importantly, I think, in terms of the nickel and dime theory of making change—provided its readers with concrete examples of people of all ages, but especially children, learning by living.

In spite of John's huge influence on so many families via his role at the helm of this revolution, I found him to be a remarkably humble man. I remember sharing with him my surprise and concern that most people who contacted me for homeschooling information wanted me to tell them what to do and how to do it, to provide them with a set of rules and procedures (and curriculum, of course) that would replace those of school. My goal was different; I wanted to help people develop the strength and self-reliance to live and learn without all of that third-party interference. John commiserated with me. And he expressed his own discomfort with the idea that people would cling to his words as to those of a celebrity or hero, and how incompatible that was with the way families have to take control of their own ideas in order to homeschool. Then, he reminded me that school conditions us for that dependence on, and comfort with, authority and hand-holding. He urged me to be patient and reminded me that change takes time. I greatly appreciated that kind, gentle wisdom (and try to incorporate it into my work to this day). As New Jersey unschooling pioneer Nancy Plent (1986, February) put it, he was a "colleague, rather than a guru" (p. 1).

That lack of conceit—accompanied by his plainspoken writing style, the anti-academic, pro-child nature of his subject, and his infectious love for children and open mind about what would make their lives better—has ensured that John's work endures. Looking back I am impressed and inspired by the way he balanced his highly original thinking and writing, and his self-description as a "man of letters," with his disdain for the academy (and the early dismissal of his work by academics). A few years ago, when I was nominated for an honorary degree (which I ultimately didn't receive), I delighted in the discovery that he had refused such an "honor" from Wesleyan University decades before, stating that colleges are among "the chief enslaving institutions" (holtgws.com/jhphotosp.2.html) in America.

But John's focus was children. His legacy was his certainty that children can and should be respected and trusted to learn, rather than being subjected to compulsory treatment by an institution. In the early days, that is what homeschooling was about. As the homeschooling movement has grown and fractured into many different camps, some of the focus on respect and trust has been lost, and some major coercion of children is now done in homeschooling's name. In addition, a whole industry has developed to provide specialized homeschool curriculum, complete with mandated projects, schedules, tests, texts, and other resources to be used by teaching parents. I do not think that is what John had in mind when he suggested that parents *Teach Your Own* (2003). Closer to what he envisioned is the term "unschooling," which he introduced to convey the need to move away from the trappings of school. From that foundation, the notion of supported self-education or open-source learning has developed and is currently taking hold at the post-secondary level, fueled by technology and the economy. That appears to be fueling a new interest in the idea of living and learning with children in the freedom that John envisioned—and is slowly, by nickels and dimes, revolutionizing education.

References

Farenga, P., Ricci, C., & Tedesco, S. (Eds.) (in press). *Growing without schooling.* Medford, MA: HoltGWS LLC.

Holt, J., & Farenga, P. (2003). *Teach your own: The John Holt book of homeschooling* (Revised ed.). USA: Da Capo Press. (Original work published 1981)

Holt, J. (2013). *Escape from childhood: The needs and rights of children.* Medford, MA: HoltGWS LLC. (Original work published 1974)

Holt, J. (1983). *How children learn* (Revised ed.). USA: Da Capo Press. (Original work published 1967)

Holt, J. (1982). *How children fail* (Revised ed.). USA: Da Capo Press. (Original work published 1964)

Holt, J. (1977, August). On social change. *Growing Without Schooling, 1*, 1.

Plent, N. (1986, February). Memories of John. *Growing Without Schooling, 49,* 1.
Preisnitz, W. (1977, August). *Natural Life Magazine, 10,* 16.
Sheffer, S. (Ed.). (1990). *A life worth living: Selected letters of John Holt.* USA: Ohio State University Press.

Wendy Priesnitz has been a book author, journalist, editor, and unschooling advocate for close to forty years. She is an agent of change who, when she was barely out of her teens, recognized the need for rethinking how we work, play, and educate ourselves in order to restore the planet's social and ecological balance. After her two daughters were born in the early 1970s, Wendy founded the Canadian homeschooling movement. She edits three magazines, including *Life Learning Magazine*, which started up in 2002 to fill the void left when *GWS* ceased publication. Her latest book is *Beyond School: Living As If School Doesn't Exist.* She lives and works in Toronto, and has two granddaughters. Her website is www.WendyPriesnitz.com.

Photographs

John Holt at the U.S. Submarine Base, New London, CT.

This photo was used for the hardcover first edition of *How Children Fail*. John Holt has his arm around Kirk Talbott; Marjo Talbott is holding Jumpy the Frog while Page Talbott observes.

John, pleased with his catch.

Berrien Moore, Strobe Talbott, Doug Talbott Jr., and John.

Photographs 67

John, an unidentified outfitter on the porch, Strobe, and Doug Talbott Jr.

John and Strobe Talbott.

John making music with Strobe's son, Devin Talbott.

Jo Talbott, Bud's wife, with John.

Photographs 69

John listening to his latest music recording, oblivious to the window washer.

A rare photo of Ivan Illich, a strong influence on Holt's later thinking about schools and society, taken by John Holt while he worked with Illich at CIDOC in Cuernavaca, Mexico, around 1970.

John and Vita Wallace. This photo, by Ed Braverman, became the cover for some editions of *Never Too Late: My Musical Autobiography*.

A slide from a photo shoot for *Never Too Late*.

John Holt and The Politics of Homeschooling

By Susan and Larry Kaseman

Among John Holt's greatest contributions are his ideas about how people learn, how grownups can help children learn, and how schools interfere with learning. Less widely recognized but equally important are his perspectives on the politics of schooling and homeschooling that continue to play a critical role in enabling families to homeschool. John provided the leadership, guidance, and direction that the fledgling homeschooling movement sorely needed in the late 1970s and early 1980s and set it on a path that continues to serve us well.

John's ideas and actions have had a strong influence on the thinking of the two of us, on our writing, and on our work to claim and maintain homeschooling freedom. We know John primarily through his writings, having met him only once, at a potluck one snowy December evening in Chicago.

In person, John was gentle, calm, and easy to approach, so we asked his advice. At that time, homeschooling was legal in Wisconsin, but because Wisconsin's homeschooling law had not yet been passed (that would take another five months), homeschoolers were concerned about the possibility of being questioned by school officials or taken to court for truancy. We knew a mother whose 10-year-old daughter was interested in many things, but not math workbooks or drills, on which she had spent little time. What could the mother say to officials if standardized tests showed that her daughter was below grade level in math? "Tell the officials she's aware of the problem and is addressing it," John responded matter-of-factly. Then, looking us in the eye, he added, "But of course you and I know this isn't really a problem." This response reflected John's confidence in children and their parents and in learning; his antipathy toward school officials, grade levels, and standardized testing; and his awareness of the need to devise practical plans to deal with public officials so children could have the opportunity be "growing without schooling."

Families who wanted to homeschool in the late 1970s faced many challenges. Homeschooling was a new idea and most people were very skeptical if not openly hostile. Despite the fact that only a few families were homeschooling, teachers and administrators, legislators, and the general public feared the impact homeschooling would have on public education. There were very few grown homeschoolers so there were very few examples of how well homeschooling works. Instead, it was unclear whether homeschoolers could succeed in college and the work force. And perhaps the most frequently asked question was, "What about socialization?"

In addition, many homeschooling families were convinced that it would be easier to stay out of legal difficulty than to have to get out of it. As a result, many homeschoolers went underground. Support groups and networks were essentially non-existent, resources were often difficult to obtain, and the Internet did not exist. John's newsletter, *Growing Without Schooling (GWS)*, addressed these issues and more. And despite the differences between homeschooling then and now, and despite John's untimely death in 1985, John's ideas were so well conceived, so basic, so prescient, that they are still relevant, helpful, and vital today.

John's contributions to the politics of homeschooling are founded on several of his unwavering convictions. These key ideas don't deal directly with the politics of homeschooling, but without them, gaining and maintaining homeschooling rights and freedoms would be much more difficult.

First, John was clearly convinced that homeschooling works. Children (and older people) can learn what they need to know without attending conventional schools. Families can help children learn and comply with the compulsory school attendance law through alternatives such as homeschooling. John (1977, August) began the first issue of *GWS* with this succinct, powerful statement:

> This is the first issue of a newsletter, about ways in which people, young or old, can learn and do things, acquire skills, and find interesting and useful work, without having to go through the process of schooling. (p. 1)

Much of John's writing describes ways in which children (and adults) learn outside of schools and provides convincing evidence that people are natural learners.

> Among the many things I have learned about children, learned by many, many years of hanging out with them, watching carefully what they do, and thinking about it, is that children are natural learners. The one thing we can be sure of, or surest of, is that children have a passionate desire to understand as much of the world as they can, even what they cannot see and touch, and as far as possible to acquire some kind of skill, competence, and control in it and over it. (Holt, 1989, p. 159)

Second, John cited powerful examples of how schools undermine learning. His determined attempts to reform schools in the 1960s and 1970s convinced him that schools are fundamentally flawed and not good places for children. John's penetrating insights into the many ways in which schools interfere with learning include the effects of schedules, standardized curriculum, testing, the social environment, and more. But he went even further in examining the destructive role that schools play in our society. For example, he wrote in *Instead of Education:*

> ... [*T*]*he schools are not failing.* They are doing what most people want them to do, and doing it very well. They know their true social tasks, functions, purposes, and they are carrying them out. The first task is to shut young people out of adult society . . . A much more important and indeed essential social function of schools is ranking—that is, grading and labeling, putting children into pecking orders, dividing them into winners and losers . . . The people who control society naturally want the schools to pick winners in such a way that the existing social order is not changed . . . The schools, then, must run a race which mostly rich kids will win but which most poor people will accept as fair. On the whole they have done this very well. [Italics in original] (Holt, 1976/2004, pp. 157–158)

Third, John helped parents develop much needed confidence that they could help their children learn despite their own doubts and disparaging comments from school officials, friends, neighbors, and the media. Holt (1977, August) wrote in the first issue of *GWS*:

> Anyway, your kids don't need, don't want, and *couldn't stand* six hours of your teaching a day, even if you wanted to do that much. To help them find out about the

world doesn't take that much adult input. Most of what they need, you have been giving them since they were born. As I have said, they need *access*. They need a chance, sometimes, for honest, serious, unhurried talk; or sometimes, for joking, play, and foolishness; or sometimes, for tenderness, sympathy, and comfort. They need, much of the time, to share your life, or at least, not to feel shut out of it, in short, to go some of the places you go, see and do some of the things that interest you, get to know some of your friends, find out what you did when you were little and before they were born. They need to have their questions answered, or at least heard and attended to—if you don't know, say 'I don't know.' [. . .] Perhaps above all, they need a lot privacy, solitude, calm, times when there's nothing to do. [Italics in original] (pp. 3–4)

In writing directly about the politics of homeschooling, John made it clear that parents have a basic right to homeschool their children. This was especially important because in the late 1970s if a family mentioned homeschooling, a common response was, "Is that legal?" John acknowledged that the state has a right to ensure that children do not grow up to be a burden on the state. But he also pointed to existing laws and court cases that support parents' right to homeschool. For example, he cited cases in which courts have ruled "Parents have a right to educate their children in whatever way they believe in" (Holt & Farenga, 1981/2003, p. 211). He also pointed out that homeschooling was not illegal under existing laws. John's ideas were particularly important because he was the first to develop publications for a national audience that stated that parents have a right to homeschool and that homeschooling works.

Through *GWS*, his book *Teach Your Own* (first published in 1981 and updated in 2003), and other writings, John provided parents with references to helpful statutes, court cases, critiques of conventional schools, and other materials they could use to support their right to homeschool. But even more important, John explained how parents could find such materials themselves, including outlining manageable steps for learning to use a law library. (Remember that neither John nor his readers had the benefit of the Internet.)

In describing how he found and used such information, John showed how parents can interpret this material for their family's use. He sent the clear, strong, necessary, and inspiring message that our interpretations as ordinary citizens are as valid as the interpretations of school officials, attorneys, and others. In fact, we need to interpret this material ourselves because other people don't have the information, perspective, understanding, and motivation that we do. The fact that our interpretations may (and often do) differ from so-called experts certainly doesn't mean that we are wrong. In fact, John often pointed out that public officials are generally biased in favor of schools and against homeschoolers, which is all the more reason we need to be skeptical of their interpretations and develop our own. Don't rely on what officials tell you the law requires, John wrote. Read statutes and court cases and interpret them yourself.

John applied his warning to even supposedly neutral interpreters, such as people who write summaries of court cases. For example, in *Teach Your Own* he urged homeschoolers to read the text of court cases themselves rather than relying on the abstracts.

In short, John's suggestions to parents for dealing with political, legal, and legislative matters paralleled his approach to ways we can help our children learn: Recognize that you have the right to do it and shoulder the responsibility yourself; recognize ways in which you are better equipped to do this than others and have confidence that you can do it. The two messages together are more powerful than either one on its own.

John's strategies were well thought out, sensible, and practical. Let's not spend time and energy trying to overturn compulsory school attendance laws, he advised. In the unlikely event that we succeeded, supporters of compulsory school attendance laws would quickly reinstate them.

John also modeled effective ways to communicate information to officials and the general public. He proceeded thoughtfully, respectfully, politely, but firmly. He explained key points in common-sense language many people could understand, whether or not they supported homeschooling. He addressed people's concerns. He assured concerned legislators that the number of homeschoolers would never be very large because few parents want to spend that much time with their children, a statement that has proven to be right on target. When people expressed concerns about parents who aren't well educated themselves and are keeping their children out of school to exploit their work, John effectively cited the old legal maxim "Hard cases make bad law." In other words, focusing on worst case scenarios results in "laws that are long, cumbersome, difficult or impossible to enforce, and far more likely to prevent good people from doing good work than bad people from doing bad" (Holt & Farenga, 2003, p. 323). However, in addressing such concerns, John didn't shy away from sharing his perspectives on the problems with, limitations of, and damage done by conventional schools.

John's key principles are very important today. Here are some of them:

- Learn by watching children. Trust them. Follow their lead and their timetable. They will show you how to homeschool.

- Remember that parents have a basic right to homeschool their children.

- Take responsibility for yourself instead of turning your life and your children's learning over to public officials. Read laws and court cases and interpret them yourself. Don't let others interpret them to their advantage and your disadvantage. Don't be afraid to come up with new ideas, new ways of looking at learning and laws.

- Think creatively. Be on the lookout for information you can use to support homeschooling or at least convince opponents that parents should be allowed to homeschool. As homeschoolers, we need to advance our own interests. Other people won't do this for us; instead they're focused on their own.

- Pick your battles carefully. John's counsel not to try to overturn compulsory school attendance laws is less relevant today than it was in the 1970s and 1980s. But the principle of carefully choosing a strategy that makes sense and has a chance of succeeding still holds.

- Use common sense. Be alert for potential allies and opponents. Ask yourself what motivates them and where you agree and disagree with them.

- Communicate in clear, straightforward language to improve the chances that others will understand what you're saying even if they don't agree with you. But also stand firm. Don't be intimidated by public officials and so-called experts and the overblown, misleading, and just plain wrong claims they often make.

- Don't attack the public schools or say things that are likely to alarm the general public and supporters of public schools. When possible, reassure opponents by reminding them, for example, that not that many people will ever want to homeschool.

- Work with other homeschoolers. Communicate with them. (Facilitating communication among homeschoolers was one of John's goals for *GWS*.) Share resources, ideas, and things that work for you.

John's writings and actions demonstrate his courage, common sense, originality, creativity, conviction, and determination. In the late 1970s and early 1980s, the emerging homeschooling movement needed to find a way to claim and maintain the right to homeschool and to counter skepticism, criticism, and strong opposition. How fortunate for all of us that John had such strong, clear perspectives about both learning and the politics of homeschooling and that he shared them so generously. Thank you, John. Thank you very much!

References

Farenga, P., Ricci, C., & Tedesco, S. (Eds.) (in press). *Growing without schooling.* Medford, MA: HoltGWS LLC.

Holt, J., & Farenga, P. (2003). *Teach your own: The John Holt book of homeschooling* (Revised ed.). USA: Da Capo Press. (Original work published 1981).

Holt, J. (1989). *Learning all the time: How small children begin to read, write, count, and investigate the world, without being taught.* USA: Da Capo Press.

Holt, J. (2004). *Instead of education: Ways to help people do things better*. Boulder, CO: Sentient Publications. (Original work published 1976)

Holt, J. (1977, August). Editorial. *Growing Without Schooling, 1,* 3–4.

Susan and Larry Kaseman have four longtime homeschooled children and several grandchildren. They lead Wisconsin Parents Association (WPA), a statewide, inclusive, grassroots homeschooling organization they helped found in 1984. WPA is committed to supporting and informing homeschoolers and maintaining homeschooling freedoms. Among Susan's and Larry's writings are many columns for *Home Education Magazine* and the book *Taking Charge Through Homeschooling: Personal and Political Empowerment*. They are grateful for the impact homeschooling has had on their lives.

Going to Court and Changing the Law for Homeschooling

By Theo Giesy

I first met John through his books. I read *How Children Fail* (1964/1982) in 1969 or 1970 when my first child, Danile, was approaching school age. It was a revelation to me. I liked school, did well, and completely missed that fear of failure and of school was a reality for many. John's description of his observations of the children in classes where he was a team teacher were wonderful and enlightening. I still assumed my kids would like school.

I also read *How Children Learn* (1967/1983) before Danile started school. My thought while reading that (and after) was, "I really like him. I would love to have him be a guest in my home and meet my children." His description of his friends' children was so like my pleasure in my children's activities that I wanted to be able to share that pleasure with him and to have my kids have the pleasure of time with John.

For Danile, liking school only lasted a month. After that the endless, pointless to her, repetition of copying off the board became mind-numbingly boring. Of course the point, for the teacher, was keeping the class occupied and quiet. Danile loved to be read to so much that I was never able to read as long as she wanted. Two hours was the longest I ever managed. So when her teacher said she had a short attention span, I was astounded.

About this time John came to do a book signing at Western Michigan University in Kalamazoo, where my husband was a math professor. I went and spent the whole time talking with him as much as I could, stepping back when others came to talk with him and stepping up when there were no others. I told him about Danile's experience in school and about the kids' activities out of school. It was just so nice to talk to someone who understood and cared. Through the afternoon I bought and had him autograph all four of the books he had written by then, I had not yet read *The Underachieving School* (1969/2005) or *What Do I Do Monday?* (1970/1995) but I wanted them because John's first two books were so good. In these later books John talks about working to try to make the schools better and talking to teachers to let them know what the parents want. He also talks about how to help your child if the school won't change. But I was optimistic.

Through Danile's first-grade year I tried working within the school system to improve things. I suggested to the teacher that more interesting activities were needed. I was told that the superintendent set policy and she couldn't change the way she ran the class. I talked to the superintendent and was told that classroom management was up to the individual teacher and he couldn't change the way the class was run. I was also told that businesses want children to be taught to do boring, repetitive tasks without question, since that is what the companies need in their employees. The situation in Danile's class improved some when the class got a student teacher to help.

Our lives paralleled John's books. We read and played games and lived our active lives. School was an inconvenient interruption, but not something that stifled learning. We also decided that ours was not a school that would change and that it would be a good idea to try to start an alternative school similar to those John described. We became part of a group trying to start a private alternative school. In Michigan the rules for K–12 schools are very restrictive. In particular, the building requirements are stricter than for a preschool or a church Sunday school. So our insurmountable problem was a location. The Unitarian church, a cinder-block building on a concrete slab floor, didn't meet the fire code for a K–12 school even though it had both preschool and Sunday school classes. That first group disbanded in frustration. A new smaller group formed the next year and found that the old Catholic high school building was usable because of a grandfather clause in the law. So in January 1973 Kazoo School opened as an alternative K–6 school with about 10 students, one certified teacher, and three other capable teachers. Danile and Darrin, ages eight and six, went to Kazoo School for the rest of that year and the next. Kazoo School is still an operating alternative school, much larger, and teaching second-generation students.

In the fall of 1974 we moved to Norfolk, Virginia. The move was quick and we didn't know how long we would stay in Virginia so we rented our house in Kalamazoo. In our move the four autographed copies of John's books were lost. Since we still had things stored in our house in Kalamazoo, I hoped to find them and I didn't replace them. So I was without John's presence in my daily life.

During our first years in Virginia, we lived in rented houses and moved every year or so. The first year, we tried public school again. Danile, now in fifth grade, had an excellent teacher, Ann, who treated her students with respect and received the wonderful results that this approach brings. Her ways of interacting with people were like the best of John's descriptions of good situations involving kids. She assumed that they were reasonable, intelligent people with needs and interests of their own who would cooperate if asked reasonably. She and I became friends and for several months Darrin could visit her class when he finished his schoolwork, approved by both teachers. So he was happy until the vice principal said that wasn't allowed. Susie got bored with kindergarten but liked it okay by attending just three days a week. So we got through that year, with the good experiences of Ann's class.

The next year we moved to Virginia Beach and the kids were in the worst school we had encountered to date. The student handbook read more like the rules for a maximum-security prison. The principal was in his first year on the job and many of the teachers, including Danile's, were also in their first year. The strongest influence was the PTA, which was composed predominately of military families of the "keep them in line, make them behave" mindset. Danile was shocked by an incident of abusive treatment of a classmate. All three of my children hated that school.

When I told Ann about the student handbook, she suggested that I write a handbook with my ideas of how the school should be. I did. She also suggested that I teach them at home. It was during this period that I found that John had written two more books *Freedom and Beyond* (1972/1995) and *Escape From Childhood* (1974/2013). I bought them and found that John's ideas had grown in the same direction as mine. In these books he went beyond talking about schooling and looked at childhood and how children are treated by society. I was thrilled to see John present the ideas of treating children as growing people, allowing them to take responsibilities as they are ready, not in a lump at 18, and to grant them the same rights in the legal system as adults. His presentation is so well thought out and explained. It was very helpful and comforting to have John's reassurance as I was dealing with people who believed that children should be treated so harshly.

I sent each child to school four days a week, allowing each a different day to stay home and have extra time with me. That lasted until December when Susie sat down in the middle of the road on the way to school and refused to go on. She walked back home and told me that the school nurse had sent her home because she had a stomachache. I was very disturbed because I knew that the nurse would not send a child home without calling first to make sure that a parent was there. I knew that she was lying and I felt that if I had taken her more seriously, she wouldn't have felt that she had to lie to avoid an intolerable situation. The school response was that it was my fault she lied because I was too lenient. If I made it clear that, no matter what she said or did, it wouldn't make a difference, she would still go to school, then she wouldn't lie because it would do her no good. I found that view horrifying.

Our family discussed the problem of school.

Kids: "Why do we have to go to school?"

Parents: "Because the law says so."

K: "Why do they have that law?"

P: "Because the state believes that people need an education."

K: "Then it is a bad law because we are not getting an education in school."

Darrin: "We learn more from you in ten minutes than we do all day in school."

K: "What would happen if you didn't send us?"

P: "They might take us to court."

K: "Could they take us away from you?"

P: "No, we could always back down and send you back to school."

K: "Okay then we want to try staying home."

That struck me as just the sort of intelligent questions and clear thinking that John describes when he talks about kids being much more able to take responsibility than they are given credit for. I received much astonished criticism for allowing children to make such an important decision. Again the support from John's books meant a lot to me.

It wasn't until they had missed thirty days of school that the authorities expressed concern about them and told us that the law required us to send them to school. That was late January and in February the kids and I went to California to be with my father for the last month of his life. He had stomach and colon cancer. Dan told the authorities that the children were not in Virginia and that ended their interest. We did not return to Virginia until mid-April. We didn't mention to the school that we were back and that took care of that school year.

After my father died, my mother gave me some money from his insurance. I used some of it to take an organic chemistry class at Old Dominion University. I also used some for ballet classes for all of us. I had always wanted to take ballet and Danile had been asking for ballet classes. She and I were the instigators, but then Susie asked if she could take it also, then Darrin asked if he could still play hockey and take ballet. We started with just one class a week each and two for Danile. Very soon the kids wanted to add more ballet classes and a drama class.

We moved to a different school district in Virginia Beach. The kids wanted to try school again. The school they had been in was so bad they thought it worth giving a new school a chance. It would have been easier to not enroll them and not make the authorities aware of them, but we were willing to try a different school on the condition that they give it at least two months. I was studying chemistry one evening and the kids asked why I was doing homework since nobody was making me do it. I replied that I was studying it because I was interested and wanted to know it so much that I had paid a lot of money to be able to take the class. I was really upset that what they were learning at school was to view studying as a battlefield where someone is trying to force you to do something and you try to do as little of it as possible to get by. That seemed to me like a very good reason to get them out of that atmosphere.

In seventh grade, Danile had a different teacher for each class and liked some of them. She had a Civil War history class that had field trips to the battlefields. She chose to remain in school for the year. She said that knowing she had a choice helped with the parts she didn't like. Darrin was soon bored and Susie was unhappy. They both wanted to leave school after two months.

Susie began to read before she started school. In kindergarten there were not many books and reading wasn't stressed, so she was still comfortable with it. When she started first grade she was so afraid of making a mistake and being thought dumb that her reading ability decreased, very much the sort of reaction that John described in *How Children Fail* (1964/1982). Her first- and second-grade teachers both talked to me about her reading. One said that she had good word-attack skills, but lacked comprehension. The other said that she had good comprehension, but poor word-attack skills. She was sitting on my lap while I was reading one of John's books aloud. I stopped to comment on what he had written. She wanted me to continue reading so she read the next several words to get me started again. Obviously her word attack skills and comprehension were fine when she felt safe.

Then John's (1976/2004) next book, *Instead of Education*, came out. Our ideas continued to grow along the same lines. He was seeing schools as bad places for children and that the best thing for parents to do was help them escape. In this book he said, "There may be no one who feels this way except me. If there are others who do, I hope through this book to find out who some of them are" (p. 201). That was very exciting to me. It meant that he would like to hear from me. Until then, I assumed that most of the people who read his books felt that way, if not from their own observations then from his writing. John's observations and ideas were so good and so clearly expressed that it seemed to me that most readers would agree with him. That statement gave me the confidence to call his office in November 1976 when we were planning a trip to New Haven to visit friends.

I called John's office and left a message referring to that passage and asking about coming to see him on that trip. I left several messages since I hadn't heard back. John called back and explained that he had been out of town. He understood that I was very eager to meet him and he said we would be welcome. We drove up in the late afternoon and visited him in his office for a couple of hours. We talked about the kids' school situation and our plans to get them out. Then I said that we would need dinner before driving back to New Haven. I asked John if he would join us and pick a restaurant. He suggested a Japanese restaurant that he liked and we had a delightful dinner and continuation of our visit. John felt to me like a long-time friend or family member. He gave the kids bites of his food and had bites of ours. It was thoroughly comfortable. After a leisurely dinner we had to head back. While we were in the office I purchased my lost Holt books and had John autograph them and the three newer ones I had brought along. After that we kept in touch by phone and letter.

We read the law in Virginia, which said: Parents must send their children (1) "to a public school," or (2) "to a private, denominational or parochial, school," or (3) have the children "taught by a tutor or teacher of qualifications prescribed by the State Board of Education and approved by the division superintendent in a home." I chose option 3 and applied to the superintendent for permission to teach them at home. That was rejected because I was not a certified teacher. I appealed because the law did not specify certified teacher. The superintendent said he would have to consult with the State Board of Education and would get back to me. I continued to teach Darrin and Susie at home. In May the superintendent rejected my request again, but the school year was over.

The money from my mother only lasted for the first year of ballet classes, so in the fall of 1977 I started working in the office at the ballet studio and as wardrobe mistress in exchange for classes. I also made costumes for pay. The kids were performing and our whole lives revolved around the ballet studio and its activities. Once we were homeschooling, reading and other school-like activities could be arranged around the ballet schedule, giving us more flexibility.

That fall we moved to Norfolk and all three kids wanted to stay home. So we just didn't enroll them. They had plenty of outside activities through ballet. Anita had reached kindergarten age. She wanted to try it even though her siblings had not liked school. So we enrolled her on November 1, right after we moved. She lasted until Christmas—and that only because she was the lead snowflake in the Christmas program and there was a field trip to see Santa. She didn't want to miss out on these activities. Kindergarten wasn't compulsory so no longer sending her wasn't a problem. All was going well until the police came to the door in the spring; I didn't know until much later that a "friend" had reported us. That was scary, but I quoted the law to them. They asked if I had applied for permission to teach at home. I said I had not because of the Virginia Beach experience. I said that I would apply to the Norfolk superintendent. They accepted that. I applied and heard nothing back so I went on as I had been. We finished that school year and started the next. We kept a low profile and reporters who inquired respected our wish to keep private. When authorities came around again we said we had applied and had not heard back. We reapplied and I spoke to the superintendent. I said that giving us permission would not cause a mass exodus from the schools, that most people want to send their children to school and that we felt that this was something extra we could do for our kids. He refused and charges were brought against us for failure to send our children to school.

I looked into what it took to open a private school in Virginia and found that Virginia has almost no regulations for private schools, only that they meet the same number of hours a day and days a year as the public schools. So we started Brook School, with our kids as the students and me as the teacher. The local newspaper wanted to talk with us; since the schools were aware of us there was no reason to keep a low profile, so we granted an interview. We were very surprised to find that we were front-page news. Our next surprise was that all the responses we got were supportive. The reaction was split between "How can we help you?" and "We'd like to do that too. How can you help us?" After we gave the first interview other reporters asked for interviews and there were several more articles. I was very pleased with our experience with the press. The articles always stuck to what I said. They did not twist or distort my words to change the meaning. All the letters to the editor were supportive. This was very reassuring to me, since the Norfolk Public Schools' reaction to enrolling our children in Brook School was not to drop the case but to press charges. Our hearing was in April 1979. Leading up to it, we were on every local talk show, and there, too, the responses were all supportive.

In a one-day hearing in which the prosecutor tried to prove that I didn't conduct school for the same number of hours a day and days a year as the public schools, all he could prove was that I was a very busy person. The judge's opinion was that leaving private schools so much leeway was a legislative choice and not an oversight, and that courts do not make law, but only rule on existing law. So he dismissed the charges. It was at the hearing that I found out who had reported us. She was there to testify against us. The schools turned to the legislature to "close the loophole in the law." This began a five-year lobbying effort that led to the Virginia Homeschooling law.

At the beginning of the lobbying effort the established private schools were represented in force saying, "Don't define or restrict private schools." They felt it was okay to stop homeschooling but not by making any laws about private schools. That slowed the legislature enough for the homeschooling movement to make its case. I took a couple of kids with me every time I went to Richmond. The legislators could see that homeschooling worked. As John says at the end of *Instead of Education* (1976/2004), we had enough evidence to convince them that this should be an option. So the lobbying continued about what form a homeschooling law should take and what requirements it should have.

Since there was so much interest in homeschooling in the area, I asked John about coming to speak. He told me that all he required was his travel expenses and a place to stay. I arranged for a room at Old Dominion University for him to speak, publicized the talk, and got an audience and enough funds to cover his travel.

At last I got my long-time wish of having John as a guest in our house. It was all I had hoped. He was the most comfortable person to have as a guest. He went along to the ballet studio with us, shared in our activities, visited with us and enjoyed what we were doing. John was someone whose good opinion mattered very much to me, and yet I never felt I had to perform, change, or show off to get it. I felt that, being myself, I had his good opinion, and that I could share ideas with him and have his understanding. To him it was as reasonable and natural as it was to me that I discussed removing the kids from school with them and that their opinion was the deciding factor. A Washington, DC TV station requested that John and a homeschooling family of his choice appear on a talk show immediately following his visit with us. He asked us to be on with him. So we got to fly to Washington, DC, the first time that the kids got to fly. We rode in a limousine from the airport to the TV studio. These were all exciting new experiences and fun for us to share with John.

Right after John's visit, we bought the house in Norfolk where we still live. For the next couple of years our involvement in ballet, local theater, and lobbying trips to Richmond kept us busy. We kept in touch with John by phone and letter, especially about lobbying. I could write John first-draft letters, so I could write to him much more than I would have if I had to proofread, edit, and copy. So I don't have copies of my letters to John.

John was also my friend and offered support for me in situations having nothing to do with school. In February 1981, the political situation at the ballet studio caused me to lose my position there and caused a rift in an important friendship. John knew how much the friendship meant to me and was sympathetic. His support meant a lot to me. Later the friendship was renewed. In the summer of 1982, my mother had treated me very badly. John said that was not an acceptable way to be treated and suggested that I should not allow it. The relationship between my mother and me did recover. John supported my great desire for another child. In response to arguments that there were too many people in the world, he said that there were not enough like my children. He included the possible future child as question marks when he autographed one of his books for me. That child, Ellen, was not born until three years after John died.

Since the homeschooling movement was growing, I felt there was enough interest to get an audience for John to do another talk so he could visit again. In October 1982, he did another talk at Old Dominion University and stayed with us. During that visit, we went to the pool at the Jewish Community Center where we had a membership. John offered the kids help as they wanted it and played with them in the water, as well as swimming himself. It was a lovely time.

The Edgar Cayce Foundation in Virginia Beach arranged for John to speak in August 1983. So I got to have him visit without doing anything. After his talk he stayed with us for a couple of days. At the end of that visit, John was going to Maryland to visit another homeschooling family, Manfred and Jeannie Smith and their children. He invited me to drive him there so we would have more time to visit and I could meet them. In these later visits, John talked of the conflict between enjoying time with friends and wanting more time for himself, especially for his music. He was tired of talking about schooling. He was ready to move on, but it was very hard to break away. We talked about his cancer. He told me of his mega-doses of vitamin C for it; when he had to have surgery, I asked about the vitamin C. He said it didn't work so well in the bottle and that when he traveled it got neglected.

John did not want to go to the hospital for the last stage of his cancer and die in the hospital. So several of his friends came to Boston to stay with him. Anita and I were there for the last ten days of his life. He was very weak and could not talk more than a word or two, but he could still enjoy having friends share their activities. We told him of the ballet programs we were putting together to perform in the schools. I showed him the pictures I had made for scenery for *Misty of Chincoteague*. One of his friends was David Chickering, a cellist on leave from the Chicago Symphony. John often enjoyed having David play for him. Our purpose was to let him be as comfortable as possible and to make sure he did not get unwanted help. He was able to decline pain medication, food, and water when he didn't want them. We made sure that his choices were honored.

At the memorial service for John, we got to meet several of his friends that we had known only from his stories. John liked to share his enjoyment so we had heard a lot about people he liked and it was nice to meet them.

What strikes me when I think about John and re-read his books is that the problems he writes about, in and out of school, still exist in pretty much the same form, and that what he had to say still applies as much now as when he wrote it. In *Instead of Education,* John (1976/2004) wrote:

> Even in the richest countries, few people still expect what not long ago they all took for granted, that they and their children will be richer in the future than they are now. In the poorer countries, most people face famine and disaster.
>
> We are beginning to move, as slowly as we can, and only because we must, into a less wasteful and destructive economy in better balance with our planet and its resources. This move takes many forms, among them depression, unemployment, poverty, and starvation. As usual, when humanity has to pay for its mistakes, the sacrifices fall most heavily on those who have the least. But people may in time demand that the sacrifices be shared more evenly, and that we make a society without winners and losers, or at least without such an enormous gulf between the two. Many who accepted that gulf when they thought they themselves had a good chance to get richer may no longer do so when that chance seems gone. (p. 210)

Those words could have been written yesterday, or tomorrow. It is discouraging that so much has stayed the same, but encouraging that his ideas are still out there to help those of us trying to do what we need to make our lives livable.

ANITA (GIESY) GOMEZ ADDS TO HER MOTHER'S RECOLLECTIONS:

I was 6 the first time John came to stay with us. He was gentle and when you talked to him he listened like he was really interested in what you had to say, whatever that was. There's a picture of me looking up at John with big adoring eyes and that was exactly how I felt. I had a teddy bear I started sleeping with shortly before his visit. It had been a family toy until I adopted him and he didn't have a name. John made such an impact on me I named the bear, John Bear—quite a compliment from a 6-year-old.

John came to visit two more times after that. It was always an exciting thing to have him come. His ability to listen and his true interest and his lack of judgment made him not only someone I could talk to, but also someone I could write to. I was a late reader and a late writer. John invited me to write to him, letting me know it was okay if it wasn't spelled correctly, and whatever I wanted to write about was fine with him. He was the only one I felt I could do this with. And he wrote back. That was also one of the motivations for working on my reading, so I could read them by myself and not have to go to my mom.

My own grandfathers died, one before I was born and the other when I was three. John became a surrogate grandfather for me. Mom was open with us in general, so I knew John was battling cancer. I heard her optimism in the early days, her worry later on. We were on a trip to CA to visit my grandmother, when word came that the end was coming. My mom decided to go to Boston and I went with her. It was the month before my 13th birthday. Because he was beloved, there were plenty of people to see to his comfort and I didn't feel there was much I could do to be helpful there, so I would go into the office of Holt Associates to help out, where I was treated with respect and appreciated. I was asked for my opinion on a set of books they thought would be good for late readers. They listened to what I had to say and took my opinions seriously; the office was the embodiment of John's ideas about how people should be treated and that kids are people, too. I have tried over the years to remember that wonderful feeling I got talking to John when I have conversations with kids, and I try to listen to them the way John listened to me.

References

Holt, J. (2013). *Escape from childhood: The needs and rights of children.* Medford, MA: HoltGWS LLC. (Original work published 1974)

Holt, J. (2005). *The underachieving school.* Boulder, CO: Sentient Publications. (Original work published 1969)

Holt, J. (1995). *Freedom and beyond.* Portsmouth, NH: Boynton/Cook Publishers. (Original work published 1972)

Holt, J. (1995). *What do I do Monday?* Portsmouth, NH: Boynton/Cook Publishers. (Original work published 1970)

Holt, J. (2004). *Instead of education: Ways to help people do things better.* Boulder, CO: Sentient Publications. (Original work published 1976)

Holt, J. (1983). *How children learn* (Revised ed.). USA: Da Capo Press. (Original work published 1967)

Holt, J. (1982). *How children fail* (Revised ed.). USA: Da Capo Press. (Original work published 1964)

Theo Giesy was born and raised in the greater Los Angeles area. She attended University of Wisconsin for four years. There she met and married Daniel Giesy. They have lived in Virginia since 1974. She enjoys traveling to California to visit her youngest daughter, Ellen, and taking trips with her grandchildren to show them the special places in the country. She remains active in causes such as climate change and food safety, particularly GMO labeling and regulation.

Anita Giesy Gomez is the fourth of Theo's children. She is married and has three children. She is a certified massage therapist living and working in Virginia.

John Holt Saved My Life
By Peter A. Bergson

John Holt saved my life.

I mean that figuratively, of course, and perhaps literally as well. He gave my life purpose and fulfillment at a time when I was emotionally at rock bottom and feeling totally adrift. He brought me to the surface, filled my lungs with air, and helped me learn how to swim.

In the spring of 1967, about to graduate from college and facing a certain invitation from my draft board to join the slaughter in Vietnam, I chose my only way out: the Peace Corps. I enrolled in a program intended to teach New Math pedagogy to old math teachers in the Philippines. After ten weeks of training in a Hawaiian sugar plantation community of 1200 Filipino immigrants, however, it became clear that the majority of my seventy-five fellow volunteers—all college graduates—didn't seem to understand the New Math concepts themselves, let alone see how to present them to others. Worse, my particular teaching style was not being well received by the host teacher, who admitted to me that she was concerned that the third graders I was working with were having too much fun and might not "settle down," to use her words, when they returned to their regular classrooms in the fall. I felt terribly stuck—constrained by the rules of the school game and, worse, threatened at the prospect of having to find some other way to avoid the draft.

I was totally confused. Wasn't the purpose of New Math to make mathematical principles both comprehensible and enjoyable?

Then lightning struck—and I mean *that* literally, too. In the midst of a summer thunderstorm, the mail brought me a copy of *How Children Fail* (1964/1982). It was sent to me by my girlfriend at the time, who was sure that I would respond well to it. What an understatement! I began reading immediately and finished the book in two days—a record for a reluctant reader like me. (I had an as-yet undiagnosed vision issue that normally caused me to fall asleep after only fifteen minutes or so of reading. But this was no "normal" book.) What caused me to power through was the basic message I took from Holt: "It ain't you, kid—it's The System."

You see, I was the classic "producer," to use John's term, as opposed to "thinker," when it came to school-related work. I went all the way through school and college with one thing in mind: Avoid that "gulp" sensation when the teacher asks you a question to which you don't know the answer. I became a master at guessing what was on the teacher's mind, what was likely to be on the next test, how to make it sound like I knew what I was talking about when all I had was the barest of knowledge in any given subject. And through it all, I was 100 percent certain that it was my entire fault that I didn't really know (let alone care about) whatever it was that I was supposed to be learning. It was my deepest, darkest secret: I was a fraud, and no one must ever find out.

And then along came this guy who said to me, "Nonsense! Not only is this not your fault; it is a crime against your humanity to instill all of this fear in you. The people who did this are at best well-intentioned and sadly misinformed; at worst, they are mean-spirited and vengeful adults who are trying to deprive you of the joy that is so sadly lacking in their own life."

I knew then and there what my life's course was going to be about. I was determined to someday start my own school, where the young people would be free to learn naturally and in the safety of a community of nurturing and intellectually stimulating adults. No tests, no grades, no forced curricula—just the opportunity to explore their interests in the company of competent and sympathetic adults.

I'll skip over the next decade to say that, at the end of it, I met the love of my life and together we founded a non-profit to practice and promote the concepts of what I now prefer to call Open Education. Along the way, we began to establish our own family, which came to include three daughters and a son. Our work included the establishment of a progressive pre-school/kindergarten program for three- to five-year-olds, informed in large part by John's subsequent writings, beginning with *How Children Learn* (1967/1983).

Then, when our eldest was about to turn five, some of the parents in our program began to ask, "What are you going to do with Amanda in the fall? Where is she going to go to school?" We truly didn't have an answer. We knew only that the regular routine of full-time traditional schooling was not up for discussion, even in a self-professed progressive independent school.

Visits to local public and private schools assured us that none of them—even the self-proclaimed progressive ones—were going to be an option. For one thing, they all demanded full-day, everyday (and night, with homework) subservience to the institution. For another, they seemed boring and focused primarily on making youths fit with the commercial culture. The way that they revered dependence on peer acceptance and trivial, pseudo-academic minutiae simply appalled us, especially given the breadth and depth of our daughter's developing young mind.

Requests from parents to extend our own program into the school-age years—at least through the elementary school level—fell on deaf ears. We saw no more value in removing other well-developing young people from *their* families for most of their waking hours than we saw in pursuing such a course for our own. Part-time group engagement seemed desirable, but virtual separation from parents and family life was out of the question. We were at a loss as to what to do for our daughter, let alone how to support other people's youths.

Once again, lightning struck. A member of our parents group came bursting in one afternoon, waving a copy of a new publication called *Growing Without Schooling* (*GWS*), practically shouting, "I've found it! I've found our answer! I know what we're going to do after OC!" by which she meant Open Connections, the name we had given to our work. And indeed she had. The magazine she was holding touted the advantages of "teaching your own" outside the confines of conventional schooling—or any other coercive environment, no matter how attractive or progressive.

"Eureka!" we thought. This mom—Madalene Murphy, who, like my wife Susan, later became a regular contributor to *GWS*—had also found *our* answer. Homeschooling (or more appropriately for us, *un*schooling) looked to be the likely path forward for our family as well as the Murphys. I couldn't wait to find out more as soon as possible.

My first response was to pick up the phone immediately and call John's office to arrange a visit. "Could John come down to the Philadelphia area to speak?" I inquired of a most cheerful and helpful Pat Farenga. "What would he think of speaking for two consecutive nights, once to the general public and once specifically to homeschoolers? What would his fee be? Would he consider staying in our home rather than being put up in a hotel?" I could barely get the words out fast enough.

All of Pat's answers were just what we wished. Thus began a multi-year friendship that culminated in a third visit from John in the months just before he died. When we went on a family trip to Boston to visit my mother, we included a stop to hang out with John in the Boylston Street office, where we enjoyed an impromptu concert complete with his cello, a plastic bugle he had lying around the office, and the Pianica that Holt Associates sold to novice music-makers (like us). Our relationship was further enhanced through our connection with Susannah Sheffer, who later became editor of *GWS* (and who eventually took the magazine to new heights in quality and purpose). At the time, Susannah was a sophomore in a nearby college who learned about our center from John's mailing list. She ended up volunteering at Open Connections two days a week for the rest of her college career as well as assisting our own youths with the development of their writing. In the process, she became a treasured family friend, which she remains to this day.

As for the specific impact of John's work on my life, beyond the initial release from the ubiquitous Great School Wounding and, later, the introduction to the concept of unschooling, it is hard to separate out what came directly from John and his writings and what came along with them through mutual explorations. Certainly the regular reading of *GWS*, and John's essays in particular, were powerful allies and reinforcements during the pioneer days of home-based education. Pennsylvania, like many states in the mid-1980s, was in the throes of renegotiating the legal requirements regarding homeschooling. The old law in PA permitted the alternative of "instruction by a properly qualified tutor . . . upon approval from the local school superintendent." This was clearly an unstable situation. It left families at the mercy of their local authorities, and most were known to be opposed to the concept of home-based education.

Thus began a three-year legislative campaign to change the law. It culminated in the last-second passage of our current regulations, literally minutes before the matter was to be turned over to the State Department of Education whose regulations were going to be far more restrictive than what we were able to secure from the legislators. With the persuasiveness of John's writings, Pennsylvania, like so many other states, was able to garner sufficient *popular* support to convince enough voters to pressure their legislators to amend the law. We could not have achieved this without comparable support from the conservative Christian community, who were far more organized and politically astute than we "secular humanists" were. But many of them acknowledged as well the validity of John's vision of youths as *natural* learners. More are still coming to adopt more of John's hands-off approach as the years have passed and conservative Christian homeschoolers have seen the limits of the school-at-home approach—limits which one of *their* leading lights, Raymond Moore, described in his books *Better Late Than Early* (1989), *School Can Wait* (1989), and *Homeschool Burnout* (1988). There is no question that having the (somewhat ironic) authority of an education "expert" like John helped us all gain the attention and respect of those in charge of The System. They may still not agree with our decision to "teach our own," but they cannot argue with the wealth of anecdotal data that *Growing Without Schooling* brought to the discussion.

Still another example of John's impact on me and mine has been the ongoing process of redefining childhood (a term which I eschew to this day because of its isolationist connotations). However, I'm not ready to go as far as John does. For example, I'm still not ready to give ten year olds the power to help elect the President. I also think John misinterpreted some key aspects of Piaget's theory and that there *are* some significant developmental differences among the ages—something which seems to be borne out by current brain research with regard to the maturation of the prefrontal cortex. I know just enough to be dangerous here; for instance, there is a stage where young children may be able to count to ten but still won't have one-to-one correspondence. They have memorized the *names* of numbers without understanding number *value*. As a result, they cannot really use math other than to fool their adoring parents into thinking they know more than they do. This leads to the false sense of security that John described well.

In fact, this, I came to realize, is what was missing with so many of my fellow Peace Corps volunteers: They didn't even understand what it meant that our number system is set in Base 10. As a result, decimals were hard to understand and as for scientific notation—forget it. In fact, as John so ably described in *How Children Fail* (1964/1982), there was a general lack of understanding of most aspects of our number system. "Double the volume? What the heck does *that* mean?"

But I digress. John's writings about alternative ways of learning and of places to engage in it (see, for example, *Instead of Education* (1976/2004), written even before he came to unschooling, also affected my thinking early on. Just as Paul Goodman's street corner reading centers opened my eyes to the restrictive paradigm of traditional schools, so, too, did John's adult education centers and the value of opening them up to young people. Similarly, his advocacy of what might be called Real Work (as we refer to it at Open Connections) for the development of both knowledge and skills was yet another contribution to my understanding of how people learn best.

Lastly, John was a supporter of two young men my age (also no longer young, alas) who designed what they called "learning/play environments" for schools and childcare centers. I had known Paul Curtis and Roger Smith from their teaching days at The Fayerweather Street School in Cambridge, MA. Later, the two of them took my place at Margaret Skutch's Early Learning Center in Stamford, CT, and began immediately to construct multi-level structures in that already-inspired physical space. The idea that young people—especially two-to-twelve year-olds—deserved a physical space that was designed especially to support people their size, by creating semi-private areas in an otherwise large and open room, and by lifting them up so they could look adults straight in the eye instead of always being one-down to them, fit perfectly with Montessori's philosophy of respect for the young. The fact that John put his stamp of approval on Paul and Roger's designs gave my interest just the encouragement I needed to experiment with this concept and subsequently make it an important component of the Open Connections approach.

I built my first environment in the living room of my own home before my wife and I found a location for our center. I have since built and/or designed a hundred more for OC, for other centers, and for individual families, including both indoor and outdoor structures for my five grandchildren. I am still so committed to the idea that I am currently revising a how-to manual that I wrote in 1984 titled *Spaces for Children*, in the hopes of replacing Hoover's goal of "a chicken in every pot" with the idea of a work/play "environment" in every home. Grandiose, I know. But if parents learn to watch closely to see how well their toddlers and preschoolers develop in their free play at home, perhaps more of them will find it easier to resist the paradigm of forced schooling later on.

I miss John terribly to this day. I cannot count the number of conversations I have had in my head in which I ask him what he thinks of this or that idea, or about the latest development in the world of compulsory mis-education. If he were alive today, would he be able to have any direct impact on current State and Federal policies? Could he be the single inspirational leader to bring together all of us old timers and young education reformers, to forge a more focused *national* response to No Child Left Behind and Race to the Top? I don't know, but I'd sure like to have the opportunity to find out. I think he would be proud—as much as his humility would have allowed, which is not much—to see what his work has wrought. Thanks to Pat Farenga and others, there's hope that his influence will only continue to grow. Someday, perhaps, we shall overcome.

References

Farenga, P., Ricci, C., & Tedesco, S. (Eds.) (in press). *Growing without schooling*. Medford, MA: HoltGWS LLC.

Holt, J. (2004). *Instead of education: Ways to help people do things better*. Boulder, CO: Sentient Publications. (Original work published 1976)

Holt, J. (1983). *How children learn* (Revised ed.). USA: Da Capo Press. (Original work published 1967)

Holt, J. (1982). *How children fail* (Revised ed.). USA: Da Capo Press. (Original work published 1964)

Moore, R., & Moore, D. (1989). *Better late than early: A new approach to your child's education.* White Plains, NY: Reader's Digest Press.

Moore, R., & Moore, D. (1989). *School Can Wait.* Washougal, WA: Hewitt Research Foundation.

Moore, R., & Moore, D. (1988). *Home school burnout.* Brentwood, TN: Wolgemuth & Hyatt.

Peter Bergson is co-founder of Open Connections, which runs a resource center for self-directed learners in suburban Philadelphia, PA (www.openconnections.org). He retired in 2009, four years after the death of his wife and fellow co-founder, Susan Shilcock. Peter and Susan parented Amanda, Emily, Julia and Nicholas Bergson-Shilcock, all of whom attended school formally for the first time when they went to college. Peter now spends at least two days a week grandparenting (he has five "grand-ones," ages one to six); the rest of the time he consults with Open Connections and chairs the Board's Development Committee. He is also a member of a small group that includes Pat Farenga who are doing their part to shift the education paradigm by way of a new website: AlternativesToSchool.com.

A Friend Who Nurtured Learning

By Patrick Farenga

When I started working with John Holt in 1981, my father made a few inquiries "to be sure this Holt guy was on the up and up." Since the first question people asked when I told them I worked for a company that advocated homeschooling was "Isn't that illegal?", Dad wanted to be sure I wasn't joining a cult or something. Dad told me that his academic contacts said John Holt was an education maverick, a radical, and a famous author; to his credit, Dad decided not to press it further since I was thriving in Boston, staying in touch with my family, and enjoying my work. When Dad did meet John Holt at my wedding a few years later, he couldn't have been more surprised by John's kind demeanor and rumpled-gentleman appearance; Dad was expecting Abbie Hoffman but got Mr. Rogers.

Many people remember John as a firebrand, and some of his most famous lines support that image. I often heard him say, "School is a place where children learn to be stupid." However, by the early seventies, John realized the sorts of changes he wanted to see were not likely to occur in schools. He had read and met Ivan Illich and his circle, and their analysis of schooling spurred John to think more broadly about children and society. As John embraced the concept of a convivial society focused on human relationships and activities, rather than a schooled society focused on consuming degrees and products, he decided not to double down and work harder within the system any more. He instead questioned why people agreed with him so much in the sixties, but didn't act upon their words when it came time to take action. His conclusion was that, deep down, people want schools to be the places they are because they believe children can't be trusted to learn anything important without being forced, bribed, or seduced by others to do so.

But John wanted to do more than shock people with words—he really wanted to do something meaningful for children's lives—and I believe he changed his tactics and strategies, but not his beliefs, to accomplish this. In the first issue of *Growing Without Schooling* (1977, August), he wrote about social change:

> If we can describe the effective majority of our society, with respect to children or schools or any other question, as moving in direction X, and ourselves, the small minority, as moving in direction Y, what I want to do is to find ways to help people, who want to move in direction Y, to move in that direction, rather than run after the great X-bound army shouting at them, "Hey you guys, stop, turn around, you ought to be heading in direction Y!" In areas they feel are important, people don't change their ideas, much less their lives, because someone comes along with a bunch of arguments to show that they are mistaken, and even wicked, to think or do as they do. Once in a while, we may have to argue with the X-bound majority, to try to stop them from doing a great and immediate wrong. But most of the time, as a way of making real and deep changes in society, this kind of shouting and arguing seems to me a waste of time. (p. 1)

I think John drew on the political and media tactics he employed in the World Federalists and progressive school reform efforts as he conceived how homeschooling could grow, but he was abandoning the party-line thinking he once embraced. For instance, John was always active in local and national politics—he worked actively for the George McGovern presidential campaign, in particular—and in the 1980s, he was interested, though not invested, in the Libertarian party. When he decided to fully embrace homeschooling he knew he was reaching an audience that was very different from his Federalist and Progressive educator days, and in the second issue of *Growing Without Schooling* magazine, John (1977, November) openly invites and supports people to cross political, social, and religious lines to unite for a common cause:

> Those who read *GWS*, and want to take or keep their children out of schools, may have very different, in some cases opposed reasons for doing this. [. . .] In all these matters, we at *GWS* have our own opinions, and will express them. This is not going to try or pretend to be an unbiased publication. We will be very biased. But we will try to be as useful as possible to *all* our readers, whether or not we agree with them on all details. And on the issue about which we are all agreed we will print as wide a range of ideas and opinions as our readers send us. (p. 8)

John's willingness to cross boundaries and engage meaningfully with people who are different from him is something that continues to inspire me, despite the fact that as homeschooling grows, it is, unfortunately, factionalizing into cliques based on how much, or how little, schooling you put your children through. It is common for Christian groups to withhold support from potential members if they will not sign a statement of faith; now the secular liturgy of schooling is showing its influence as some homeschooling support groups refuse to let members join until their educational and social backgrounds have been vetted. John despised this labeling and sorting in school; to me it is a most unfortunate, though not unexpected, development in homeschooling/unschooling. Nonetheless, as long as homeschooling keeps growing I have hope, as John did, that more and more people will want, in John's (1983, December) words, "a life worth living and work worth doing—that is what I want for children (and all people), not just, or not even, something called 'a better education'" (p. 266).

Though John did find a life worth living and work worth doing, he had some regrets about how things turned out for him. The alternative therapies, changes of diet, and finally conventional surgery couldn't prevent John's melanoma from spreading, and after months of fighting cancer, John accepted that he was dying and asked me to retrieve all the items from his safe deposit box. When I returned, we sat together in my office at Holt Associates, as we often did, with John in a comfortable black, leather chair and me seated behind my desk. I busied myself with work while John went through the items I had brought him. He picked up a fancy ring that belonged to his grandmother and, after a few minutes, tears fell from his eyes as he looked it: "No engagement for Johnny," he cried.

Reporters sometimes asked John why he never married and had children and he usually replied, "Well, it wasn't because I didn't try." To say John was unlucky in love only covers part of the story; he was also driven to take action that ran against cultural norms and that could make him seem eccentric to people. For instance, he lived in a very expensive section of Boston (though Beacon Hill was more of a cultural creative enclave when he purchased his unit there in the 1960s), and, much to the consternation of his fellow condo owners, John maintained a compost heap on his balcony where he would raise worms to help improve Boston's soil. In a profile of him done by Mel Allen (1981, December) in *Yankee* magazine, John said,

> My actions sometimes are on the edges of some kind of normal distribution curve and I guess that's what eccentric means. But they are not queer or nutty. My

actions are eminently sensible. We have to save water and turn waste into soil. It's my contribution, however small, to a situation I can't do much to change.

This ability to connect small personal actions to the larger social changes one desires is something John taught that resonates even more as I age and witness increasing political and institutional gridlock in society. When I first met John, I thought the way society changed is for a political party or institution to advocate for change, led by a charismatic spokesperson and campaign, and then organize individuals to form a block of voters to support this effort at the ballot box. That's what I was taught in school as democracy in action. But John and many of the people and writers he introduced to me saw that social change under this model was no longer working and proposed other ways to conceive social change, especially by making the change you want in your own life first, thereby serving as a model for others to do so.

Another eccentricity of John's, also noted in the *Yankee* (1981, December) magazine article, was his habit of cleaning up the city as he walked around it. There were not many laws or incentives for returning empty bottles then, and John was very annoyed by the garbage he encountered as he walked around town (he gave up owning a car in the city years earlier). So he picked up as much trash as he could as he walked, sometimes appearing at the office with a bag full of empty bottles and refuse. When I asked him why he did this he replied, "Boston is my city and I don't like my city to be dirty."

Whenever I hear critics of Holt's ideas claim homeschooling is isolationist, secessionist, or elitist, it makes me wonder what they are basing this on; it certainly isn't in Holt's writing, beliefs, and actions. Yes, there are others in the homeschooling movement who match that description, but that isn't John nor was it ever part of his motivation for encouraging parents to teach their own children. Balancing the tension of the individual versus the group, being me and also being us, is a serious issue that John explored in his work and shared with others in his personal life. John decided to trust people to make up their own minds and take action, whereas many of our experts, laws, and institutions seek to usurp that authority under their mission to care for people by doing something to them for their own good. This is a tricky business, and one that society needs to address better than we are doing now as individual rights are increasingly constrained by institutional demands.

Once he was diagnosed with cancer, John decided to spend even more time playing cello and enjoying music. John liked big band music, especially Charlie Barnet and jazz in general, but his passions were classical music and the cello. For a period in the 1970s, it was common to find John playing his cello during the early morning hours in the Boston Public Gardens. One of his prized possessions was a Travielo, an electric cello that broke down for easy travel. After he purchased it he instructed me to book his travel by trains rather than planes whenever possible so he could play his Travielo en route.

John and I shared an enthusiasm for music (we once hummed Harry James' entire trumpet solo from "Sing, Sing, Sing" together), and he gave me one of the greatest gifts I ever received: my instrument rental and ten lessons to learn the tenor saxophone. John asked for nothing in return but I felt weird taking such a gift from him, so I suggested that in exchange I write a series of articles for *Growing Without Schooling* magazine about learning to play an instrument as an adult beginner. The saxophone continues to be an emotional and artistic outlet for me, and I think of John every time I touch it. If John was speaking with you or on the phone, you might see his left fingers moving up and down the penholder in his breast pocket—he was practicing his cello fingerings. He told me that he felt he brought more joy and happiness to people through sharing his music than he did from his writing, because his music didn't cause harsh disagreements.

John was also an avid audiophile: he collected records (middle European and Scandinavian composers were his favorites) and was a devoted subscriber to the Boston Symphony Orchestra (BSO). Though he enjoyed attending many concerts each year, John tried never to miss the rehearsals of the BSO. He found the rehearsals fascinating, plus he received permission to record them for his personal use only. The morning after a BSO rehearsal, John would come into the office and share his latest recordings with me, marveling at how, by using two microphones crossed over each other and mounted on a short stick, he achieved a better recording than professional recordings he owned. He would evaluate the music recorded on his Sony Walkman Pro as if he were a record producer. When John was on the road speaking, which was often, he gave me his BSO tickets for the dates he would miss. John didn't like to waste anything, particularly good music, and I, too, soon enjoyed watching the rehearsals almost more than the concerts.

John read an awful lot of books each week, as well as a select group of publications he subscribed to. He didn't subscribe to newspapers anymore, but I did, so he would often grab my morning paper when I came in and read it in a chair near my desk, sometimes commenting on what he read. In hindsight, I know I am very fortunate that he spent so much time talking seriously with a young person, especially since I had a lot to get up to speed with in order to hold up my end of the conversation. As I continued to work at Holt Associates/Growing Without Schooling and move up the ladder of corporate responsibility I was lucky to have John sitting there talking with me each day about all manner of things: education, the news, personal matters, business, politics, books—books! Oh, could we talk about books.

We shared our favorite books and authors with each other; of course, John introduced me to many I had never known about. But I'm happy to say I knew some authors John hadn't read and that he enjoyed, such as Canadian author Robertson Davies; when John decided to add a few of Davies's novels to the John Holt Book and Music Store, I felt honored. Davies's big-hearted portrayals of people allow him to create empathy in the reader even for his villains, and I think this appealed to John's own big heart. For instance, John knew all the panhandlers on his walk to and from the office, and rather than ignore them, he gave them each a quarter every time he walked by. When I asked if he thought the street people were using him since they knew he was a steady, easy touch, John replied that he didn't think of it that way. He never felt a need to ask why someone was begging for money or what they would do with it when he gave it to them, because if they had to beg for money, a difficult and distasteful thing to do, then that was all he needed to know to help them. John cited his grandmother as his example for this behavior; during the Great Depression, she provided food without question to anyone who came by her house and asked for it.

John was a close observer of children in and out of the office during the time I knew him. One thing John did for many years, and that he lamented having to curtail, was watching children in playgrounds and parks. In the early 1980s the faces of missing children were being placed on milk cartons and child abduction fears were fanned by the media; John told me that he was now being viewed very suspiciously by parents when he sat alone on a park bench watching children play, so he brought a book or newspaper to hide his face while he sneaked peeks at the scene before him. Fortunately, the many children coming into the Holt Associates office in those days provided John with plenty to observe. On a few occasions at the office, I saw John walking behind a young child and narrating their exploits into his tape recorder for later reference.

But one thing very young children do that cut right through John was their loud crying. I remember a mother who came to our office and whose baby, around 9 to 12 months old, was crying inconsolably and it was wearing on John. He couldn't take it anymore so he walked up to the baby, who was being held in his mother's arms, looked him square in the eyes, and bawled until the baby stopped and looked at John in disbelief. John nodded at the child and said, "That's what its like, do you see?" That was actually the only time I saw John do anything like that with a child; his usual practice was to put on his hearing protectors and continue working. John's hearing protectors were the same ones used by airport personnel on the tarmac; he wore them to protect his ears from the constant noise of Boston's streets and from the noise in the office when he wanted to write. John decided to sell them in our catalog to help parents stay calm and focused when they are near children's raucousness or emotional outbursts. They do not block all the sound, but they do lower the volume considerably, and for people with sensitive ears like John's, that was a big help. Indeed, this tradition continues in my life as my wife, now a teacher in a charter school, uses these hearing protectors successfully in her school as a way for the kids to block out auditory distractions while they work in class.

When his life was drawing towards its end, John told me that what bothered him the most was not knowing what my children, or Donna Richoux's children, would be like (Donna took over for John as editor of *GWS*). That always stuck with me: He wasn't worried how Donna and I would handle his legacy, he was wondering about our families on his deathbed.

A self-described late bloomer, John consistently shows in his writing and music that it is never too late to change and try something new. I know this is easier said than done, but the point is at least to try. John spent years thinking about schools and society before he decided to embrace homeschooling as a hopeful path for education. He knew not all homeschoolers shared his reasons for homeschooling, but he decided to see where this path led and to help blaze it. He said that how society treats children teaches them more important lessons than school classes do, which is why John wanted to figure out how to reintegrate children into society, so they could show us what people, places, and things can help each child flourish. This spirit of trust in the individual is not just for children, but for all people, and that is why I think John was willing to trust and hope that, no matter what mixed allies homeschooling creates, we can work it out better together than alone or as rivals.

References

Allen, M. (1981, December). The education of John Holt. *Yankee Magazine*.

Farenga, P., Ricci, C., & Tedesco, S. (Eds.) (in press). *Growing without schooling.* Medford, MA: HoltGWS LLC.

Holt, J. (1977, August). On social change. *Growing without Schooling, 1*, 1.

Holt, J. (1977, November). Mixed allies. *Growing without schooling, 2*, 8.

Holt, J. (1983, December). To Susannah Sheffer. In Sheffer, S. (Ed.), *A life worth living: Selected letters of John Holt.* USA: Ohio State University Press.

Patrick Farenga began work at Holt Associates in 1981 and became publisher of *Growing Without Schooling* magazine in 1985, when Holt died, until 2001, when it ceased publication. Farenga continues to write books and articles about learning outside of school, as well as speak at and organize conferences and seminars about homeschooling, unschooling, and Holt's ideas. He also appears on national television and in the news as a homeschooling expert. Farenga is the coauthor of *Teach Your Own: The John Holt Book of Homeschooling* and operates the website www.JohnHoltGWS.com. He and his wife have three daughters who were unschooled and are now adults.

What I'm Left With

By Susannah Sheffer

I arrived in Boston a few months after John died. Both his office and his apartment were still much as he had left them, and as I was learning the ropes in those first weeks of work at Holt Associates, I also helped out with the enormous task of sorting through John's papers and other material. I had been invited to help carry on the work of Holt Associates; I felt as if I were also being invited into the grief that surrounded the work in those days, particularly for John's close friends and colleagues who had been so much a part of his illness and dying.

Despite the grief, it was where I wanted to be. I was thrilled to be learning the work of editing *Growing Without Schooling*, the unusual little magazine that John had founded years before, and I was thrilled to be allowed to delve into the files of John's papers, especially the hundreds of letters he had written over the past decades. I had known John mostly through letters, and one of the many treasures in the big cabinet of correspondence files was my own stack of handwritten pages to John that I hadn't reread since I had mailed them to him as a young teenager.

Because our correspondence had meant so much to me, and because I understood by then that I was only one of many correspondents, I suspected that there would be enough material in John's files to make a book of letters. The idea of a letters book had come to me just hours after I'd gotten the news of John's death, and now, in Boston, as I was learning about the magazine and all the other work of Holt Associates, I was continuing to nurture the hope that I might get to make that book idea happen, even as young as I was and with no book credits to my name.

It took two years to find a publisher, so I had a lot of time to work at keeping that hope alive. My pleasure in the letters themselves sustained me: reading them, typing every word and feeling John's prose in my own fingers, thinking about themes, tracking down all the explanatory details.

Because I like this kind of symmetry, and because John had written so vividly about his daily walk from his Beacon Hill apartment to the office on Boylston Street, I would sometimes take a stack of John's letters and work in a café on his street corner. The café was called *Il Dolce Momento,* the sweet moment, and that too reminded me of John.

Sometime later I wrote a poem called "In Boston," set in that café. The poem opens:

> Here in your city
> in a cafe called *Il Dolce Momento*
> I order rich cocoa
> for its stubborn sweetness
> on the tongue, for the way it defies grief
> so boldly.

After musing for several more lines about the work of editing the letters, about John's death, and about the Boston landscape, the poem ends:

> We are what we are left with
> so I am this sweet moment
> and the way I wrap my hands around it,
> refusing to be distracted
> from my own survival.

It's staggering to realize that 25 years have passed since that scene. I'm thinking about the line "we are what we are left with," thinking about John's legacy to so many people and his specific legacy to me: What he left me with that I still carry today.

John left me the gift of audacity: The daring to reach out to someone, or reach for a new idea or project, even if there might not be an obvious protocol for doing it. If I had understood or thought too much about the possibility that John Holt, a highly regarded writer and thinker, had hundreds of people writing to him, I wouldn't have written him my first letter at age 14, telling him that I had read his books and agreed with what he said. The powerful connection I felt with his work, and the lack of others around me who felt the same way, propelled me into that initial letter, but it was John's own example that inspired me to reach out to so many other people whose work or ideas I admired over the subsequent years.

One of the previously unpublished fragments we found among John's (1971) papers was a passage about finding one's teachers. It has these lines:

> One might say that one of our important life tasks was to
> find our true teachers, to make our own university [. . .]

> Certainly to find one of one's own teachers, someone from whom we think we can learn something really important, is one of the really great pleasures of life. (p. 15)

I loved the active stance that this implied, and John's recognition of the distinct pleasure of the learner–teacher connection. John seemed to write to or call up anyone from whom he felt he had something to learn. Sometimes this led to a one-time exchange of information; sometimes it led to a long-term friendship. Of course, sometimes he must have gotten no response at all. That's a risk of this kind of audacity.

John also gave me, as he gave so many people, the gift of trust. When I was a teenager writing to him about the challenge of going to school and disagreeing with so much of what went on there, John responded, "I sympathize very strongly with you, being in the middle of it. . . . I wouldn't waste a lot of energy in fighting school. Save it for the important parts of your life."

Even as I read that letter, I knew that doing what he advised was not going to be easy, and indeed it never was. Saving it for the important parts of my life while continuing to go to school every day—and while living in a world that thought school *was* the important part of any young person's life—was challenging right up until I graduated from college. But it was amazing to me that John could make the distinction between school and my real work, could encourage me to make it too, and never doubted which was more important.

As I got a bit older, John was sometimes tougher, though no less caring, as he responded to my struggles. When I'd written him yet again about the challenge of being in school (by this time, I meant college) and feeling conflicted about it, John (1983, December) quoted to me his favorite proverb: "'Take what you want,' says God, 'and pay for it.'" He added:

> The three great arts of life are (1) Finding out what you truly want (2) Finding out what it costs (for it always costs something), and how by thought and skillful bargaining you can reduce that cost to a minimum (3) When you have found the lowest possible cost, *paying it without complaining.* Very hard for people to do, and #3 hardest of all. (p. 265)

Sometimes I wished that John were more overtly sympathetic to the tensions I inhabited during those years, but he was giving me the gift of a particular kind of aspiration, challenge, and faith. It seemed he was always prodding me toward greater integration or at least greater ownership of whatever I chose. Once he suggested that I rip up my end-of-semester grades rather than look at them. I had been telling him that I found it almost impossible to insulate myself from the cascade of feelings that grades (whether good or bad) engendered in me, despite—or maybe because of—how deeply I disagreed with them as a method of evaluation. His suggestion was, again, audacious and in its own way truly sympathetic to my experience. It was a way of saying: You're not as stuck as you think. There are other ways, wherever you are. Figure it out, do what you need to do or what you feel you can do, but do *something*. (I did rip up my grades without reading them that semester. Eventually I stopped working in places where I had to receive or give grades, which was even better.)

I met John in person only a handful of times, and each is still vivid in my mind. Our last visit was at the home of Peter Bergson and Susan Shilcock and their children in Bryn Mawr, Pennsylvania. I had found the Bergson-Shilcock family through the pages of *Growing Without Schooling* and we had become close friends and colleagues. When John came to visit in May of 1985 he was, I think, making the rounds of various friends and saying goodbye, though I didn't understand that at the time. What stays with me is the vibrant undercurrent of connection that we all felt, which is captured a bit in these lines of another poem of mine:

> . . . our last meal together, holding hands around the table
> with friends. He said *I feel a pulse
> but can't tell whose it is*, the hosts served warm bread,
> raw peas, the children left the table to chase fireflies
> on the grass, begged *catch me* as they dove into handstands,
> slapping their cool ankles against our palms.

I remember John's stories as we all stayed up late into the night talking. I remember listening as Peter and John recalled their young adult years and remarked that influences during those years could be quite lasting. "So watch out," they said to me, jokingly making fun of themselves as they acknowledged the company I was keeping at that very moment. I laughed with them and knew, as they must have too, that I couldn't have been luckier.

That spring, Peter was trying to convince me to take on the job of editing the local homeschooling newsletter, and when he enlisted John's help in persuading me, John looked me in the eye and said, "I think you'd make a great editor."

I remembered that moment frequently over the next few years, when I was in Boston working with the others at Holt Associates. John trusted our ability to carry on his work, and we had to learn to trust ourselves, which meant maintaining a sometimes subtle combination of honoring history and forging new paths. Soon after I started work at Holt Associates, I came across a passage that seemed so relevant to our own challenges that I copied it out and stuck it on the wall. It was a passage in the book *Summerhill: For and Against*, a collection of essays about A.S. Neill and the school he founded. In John's essay, he wrote:

> The worst thing that can happen to any great pioneer of human thought is for his ideas to fall into the hands of disciples and worshippers, who take the living, restless, ever-changing thought of their master and try to carve it into imperishable granite, so that not a word shall ever be lost or changed. The words may remain, but the spirit is soon lost. A friend of mine used to say, "A conservative is a man who worships a dead radical." Nowhere is this more true than in education; one thinks immediately of Maria Montessori and John Dewey. It would be a tragedy if it happens to Neill. The only way to prevent it, to honor Neill as he deserves, is to try to continue the exploration he started, to move on further into the uncharted territory of human freedom, happiness, and growth. (p. 97)

It would be a tragedy if it happens to Holt. Knowing one's intellectual history is crucial, of course, and in the 1990s I had the opportunity to edit the Innovators in Education series at Boynton-Cook/Heinemann, for which we brought back into print a great line-up of radical education classics so that contemporary readers could know them, learn from them, and trace the connections between that canon and the work currently being done. I admit to feeling irritated when people seem to disregard this heritage or, worse, assert something about Holt without having read his work. But I feel just as powerfully the truth of what John wrote about Neill and what I take as a reminder about his own legacy: we honor him by continuing, and by moving forward in our own ways, into the territory that he began to explore during his lifetime.

Sometimes I think I feel John's influence the most when I'm engaged in work that appears least directly connected to his. In the years since *Growing Without Schooling* ceased publication, I have continued to work closely with young people through my own particular blend of writing work, therapeutic listening, mentoring, and other nuances that make it hard to describe with an easy label. I work part-time at North Star: Self-Directed Learning for Teens, which makes growing without schooling available to teenagers who wouldn't otherwise have felt able to choose it. Some days, as I'm running up the stairs at North Star to my next appointment with a teenager, I think about how much John would have loved what North Star is doing.

But a lot of my creative interests these days are in what look like other realms. I've worked for the past twelve years on the staff of an organization of family members of murder victims and family members of people who have been executed. I've written a book in collaboration with a man who spent time in prison titled *In A Dark Time: A Prisoners Struggle For Healing And Change* (2005), and another book titled *Fighting For Their Lives: Inside The Experience Of Capital Defense Attorneys* (2013) about the emotional experience of capital defense attorneys who have lost clients to execution. I didn't think or write about prisons, victims' family members, or the death penalty at all for most of my years at Holt Associates, and now these subjects occupy a huge part of my mental landscape.

At least in my own mind, there are a lot of overlaps between these areas of work. My husband Aaron Falbel says that the nexus is in the belief that *how we treat people matters*. I agree that that's a great and succinct summary of what my education and criminal justice interests have in common. When I say that I feel John's influence, though, I mean a couple of other things as well.

For me, John's work was so much about paying attention to people's subjective experience. What is school like for kids? Sitting in the classroom observing and making the notes for what would become the book *How Children Fail*, John kept asking that question and paying attention to the actual answer, the answer that was close to the ground of experience rather than to a lofty belief about what school might be like or ought to be like. And because he paid that kind of attention, he was able to write what he saw in a way that let others—including the fifth grader I was when I first read *How Children Fail*—connect with it. Today, whether I'm listening to a teenager or to a capital defense attorney, the question that gets me quickest to the heart of what I am interested in learning is: *What is it like?* What is it like to be you, to do what you do, to go through what you have gone through?

I also felt John's influence keenly when I first got involved with this newer work and was instantly way outside my zone of familiarity, comfort, and, at first, competence. I had to tolerate a great deal of not-knowing and not-understanding, and I had to try *not* to resort to all the defensive and self-protective strategies that John had described so well. I also had to trust in my own sense of what was compelling and what I most wanted to learn at that point in my life—and to let that be the reason to pursue whatever new project I was pursuing.

I've written about a few gifts from John, and I could just as easily have written about several others instead. I think often of all that I'd love to tell John now, and ask him. At the same time, I treasure what he left me with. It's a rich legacy.

References

Farenga, P., Ricci, C., & Tedesco, S. (Eds.) (in press). *Growing without schooling.* Medford, MA: HoltGWS LLC.

Hart, Harold, ed. (1970) *Summerhill: for and against.* New York: Hart.

Holt, J. (1983, December). To Susannah Sheffer. In Sheffer, S. (Ed.), *A life worth living: Selected letters of John Holt.* USA: Ohio State University Press.

Holt, J. (1982). *How children fail* (Revised ed.). USA: Da Capo Press. (Original work published 1964)

Holt, J. (1971). Notes for talks to students. *Growing Without Schooling, 60,* 15.

Sheffer, S. (2013). *Fighting for their lives: Inside the experience of capital defense attorneys.* Nashville, TN: Vanderbilt University Press.

Sheffer, S., & Harrison, D. (2005). *In a dark time: A prisoner's struggle for healing and change.* Sunderland, MA: Stone Lion Press.

Susannah Sheffer edited *Growing Without Schooling* magazine and the book collection of John Holt's letters, *A Life Worth Living,* and she has written other books and articles about homeschooling, teaching, and learning. She works with young people at North Star: Self-Directed Learning for Teens in Hadley, Massachusetts and is on the staff of the nonprofit organization Murder Victims' Families for Human Rights. Her latest book is *Fighting for Their Lives: Inside the Experience of Capital Defense Attorneys.*

A Man Who Saw Things Clearly

By Aaron Falbel

Most, if not all, of the pivotal turning points in my life were the result of chance encounters. Such was the case with my meeting John Holt, who was to have a decisive influence on my life at a crucial juncture.

In April 1984, I found myself working as a research assistant to a professor at MIT known for his radical ideas on education. (He spoke of "natural learning," "learning without a curriculum," "learning without being taught," and so on.) A year earlier, a presidential commission called the National Commission on Excellence in Education issued a report titled *A Nation at Risk: The Imperative for Educational Reform* (1983, April). The report opened with these ominous words:

> Our Nation is at risk. [. . .] the educational foundations of our society are presently being eroded by a rising tide of mediocrity that threatens our very future as a Nation and a people. [. . .]
>
> If an unfriendly foreign power had attempted to impose on America the mediocre educational performance that exists today, we might well have viewed it as an act of war.

That America's schools were failing was nothing new. Presidential commissions dating back to the 1940s, if not earlier, had said the same thing. But the report's analysis and recommendations did not ring true to me. It advocated more school: longer hours, higher standards, better pay for teachers, and so on. It seemed to me that a more radical understanding of the issue was needed, and that more school was unlikely to improve matters. The professor I worked for agreed and felt that he had to respond to this report in some way. "Go find out what is *really* wrong with the schools," he told me. So I trotted off to the Humanities Library and went to the stacks to read whatever I could on educational criticism. One title caught my eye immediately: a book called *How Children Fail* (1964/1982) by someone named John Holt. "Ah, just what I'm looking for!" Nearby was another title by the same author, *Instead of Education* (1976/2004). I put that book in my growing pile as well. I gathered up a few other titles and went home to read them.

The two titles by Holt blew me away. Here was a guy who pulled no punches. He dared write what few other authors had the courage to say: *The emperor has no clothes; schools are a sham. The way they are designed actually thwarts learning. Their structure sabotages curiosity and inquisitiveness and directs children's mental energies into defending themselves against the endless barrage of pedagogical intrusions.* He had the rare, uncanny ability to see into the minds of schoolchildren and practically read their thoughts and feelings.[1] He could see the debilitating effects of fear and anxiety on their ability to use their minds well. This led him ultimately to conclude: "School is a place where children *learn* to be stupid" (1964/1982, p. 263).

In *Instead of Education* (1976/2004), Holt gave a glimpse of what things could be like if schools gave up their mission of people-shaping and became resources for doers. This resonated strongly with my own experience: I felt that school was essentially a game that one had to play, whereas real learning had to do with one's genuine interests and passions. (Quite frequently, the former got in the way of the latter.) Moreover, I noticed that in the revised edition of *How Children Fail* (1964/1982), Holt quoted the professor I was working for, several times. I went back to the professor and asked, "Do you know this guy named John Holt? What he is saying is absolutely amazing and dovetails nicely with your own perspective on things." He replied, "Oh, yes. John Holt. I know him. He might be a good person to talk to. Some of his best writing is contained in the magazine he publishes, *Growing Without Schooling*."

I found out that Holt Associates still had an office in downtown Boston, on Boylston Street. I was told by someone who knew Holt (a homeschooling parent, as it turned out) that he was an approachable man and would be glad to meet with anyone who took his ideas seriously. (I surmised from this comment that there were many who didn't.) I was determined to meet the man, but first I had to prepare myself by reading through *all* his books, as well as complementary books by Dennison, Herndon, Neill, Goodman, and Illich. The more I read of Holt, the more impressed I became with the simple clarity, honesty, and integrity of his words. John Holt's writing had the ring of truth. He, more than anyone,

---

[1] Norm Lee, a friend of John's, once quipped that John Holt could just as well have titled his first book *How Children **Feel**.*

knew "what was wrong with the schools." I took his work seriously, all right.

I finally arranged a meeting with John in his third floor office on a very hot day in August. He was casually dressed, in shorts and a T-shirt, and he had a small hand towel draped over his leg, not very discreetly hiding what seemed to be a large growth on his thigh. We hit it off right away. We talked about many things: the primary and secondary purposes of schooling,[2] his experiences in the school reform movement, the latest craze over educational technology, and we also talked a lot about music. (I played classical chamber music semi-professionally at the time.) I asked many questions about the Bagsværd Ny Lilleskole, the Danish school about which he wrote in *Instead of Education*[3] (1976/2004). I asked whether Peggy Hughes, who made a film about the Ny Lilleskole, *We Have to Call It School*[4] (1974), was still available to show her film and lead a discussion about it, thinking that the folks at MIT would be interested in this. John said that he thought that this could be arranged and remarked that he hadn't seen the film in years and might be interested in coming if I arranged a showing. I could hardly believe my ears. Eventually, a screening was arranged and both John Holt and Peggy Hughes attended. In the end, I was wrong about the MIT people; they weren't that interested in the Ny Lilleskole. I, on the other hand, was *very* interested, and this so-called "school" was to play a major role in my life—but that's another story.

Even before viewing the film, John and I had many more conversations. I was floored by the clarity of his thought and acuity of his vision. I remember one conversation where we were talking about the "bottling plant metaphor" that figured prominently in an article Holt recently wrote for *The Progressive* ("Why Teachers Fail," 1984, April, pp. 32–33). I said casually that this reminded me of the motto of a certain progressive school in Texas, the Lamplighter School: "A student is not a

---

[2] Holt wrote in a letter to John McDermott in 1977: "I have spoken of the primary and secondary purposes of schools. Secondary purposes are all those things about democratic values, cultural tradition, communication skills, critical thought, best that man has thought and done, etc. The primary purposes are (1) to keep kids out of the adults' hair, (2) to grade, rank and label them, (3) to prepare them for life as mass producers and consumers. Most teachers don't even like to think about those primary purposes. Some teachers understand that they exist, but think that they can carry out the secondary purposes anyway. The hard fact is that the primary and secondary purposes cannot be carried out in the same institution, they are altogether incompatible." See *A Life Worth Living: Selected Letters of John Holt*, ed. Susannah Sheffer, Ohio State Univ. Press, 1990, p. 208.
[3] See Chapter 11, "One of the Best S-chools."
[4] This excellent film can now be viewed on YouTube.com.

vessel to be filled, but a lamp to be lighted." Without missing a beat, John said, "I've heard of that place, but they've got it all wrong. Their lamps are *already* lit. They just need to stop doing the types of things that blow them out." I was humbled. Here was a man who saw things very clearly, indeed. (How naïve I was back then!)

I remember talking with John about the term "learning environment," a favorite phrase of the MIT crowd. John didn't go for it. "*All* environments are learning environments," he insisted. "We don't need to create or design special places where something called 'learning' happens. I don't make any distinction in my own life between learning and other pursuits." In a piece Holt (1974, April 8) wrote called "Imagining the Future: The Learning Society . . . " and again, later, in his book *Teach Your Own* (1981/2003), John came to question the usefulness of talking about "learning." He preferred to speak of concrete activities, of *doing*.

And I had still more questions about the Ny Lilleskole. I could tell John had a certain soft spot in his heart for the place, but in many ways, he had moved far beyond it. Perhaps he was starting to get a bit impatient with my questions about it when he turned to me one day and said, "You know, as nice as the Ny Lilleskole was and is, you have to realize that it is an *artificial* place." I had to admit that he was right. The real challenge was not to make nice little places for kids to be in, but to make the world—our homes, communities, and workplaces—as welcoming and hospitable to young people as we possibly can. As Holt put it, as far back as 1971, "There cannot be little worlds fit for children in a world not fit for anyone else" (as cited in Graubard, 1974, p. 267).

Indeed, we talked a lot about what John felt was the futility of school reform. At the time, I was something of an agnostic about this. The image of the Ny Lilleskole captivated my imagination. I knew the odds were against making meaningful changes in schools, but I did not have John's long and bitter experience in this regard. In a letter Holt wrote me after one of our conversations, he stated,

> The possibility of making humane changes in schools in any foreseeable future seems to me microscopic, infinitesimal. It is not an accident that schools are what they are. For many years I used to believe, and hope, that schools and the people in them would act more wisely and humanely if only someone suggested to them a way to do so. I have discovered by what I think I can fairly call bitter experience that they reject, and angrily reject, these more humane and intelligent ideas whenever they are presented to them. School, for the people in it, is first

> and foremost an institution in which they are able to exercise power over other people. They are much closer in spirit to police or prison guards than to educators in any real sense of the word. The overwhelming majority of teachers, certainly well over 90%, resist with all their strength any proposal for changes in schools which would diminish the power they have over their students. That humane minority, some of whom are always there, usually does not stay in schools for long, mostly because they cannot stand to do the things they are told to do, or to be around the kind of people they have to be around. We are talking here about something that goes much deeper than merely mistaken ideas. We are talking about defects of character. This is not a thing I say in public, because it would not do any good, but in private I can say to you that I am absolutely sure of it. (J. Holt, personal communication, September 10, 1984)

And in another letter, in which John was discussing the prospect of convincing teachers to give their students more freedom of choice in their classrooms, he stated,

> I have been trying to convince teachers of this, as I say, for 25 years, and I have had very little luck. I say that when you give up the attempt to control everything in the classroom and think of yourself as a guide or facilitator, your work becomes much more rewarding and effective. Teachers do not want to hear this, and refuse to hear it. That control, that power, is meat and drink to them, the breath of life. They do not dare run the risk that if they gave this up they might in time reach some other kind of relationship with children, and in any case they are realistic enough to know that if they did, they would probably be in trouble, as I was in trouble. (J. Holt, personal communication, September 1, 1984)

I dwell on this point because in the years following these conversations, I have encountered this bitter truth over and over again, and not just within the sphere of education reform. The unwillingness to give up control seems to rear its ugly head in any situation in which one group of people has power over other people (or over other living beings): in issues of war and peace, in the criminal justice system, in matters of economic justice, in the exploitation and degradation of the environment, in matters pertaining to economic and technological development . . . the list goes on. We cannot seem to let go of our power and control *even when* the exact nature of the harm that we do is pointed out to us. As John saw, this is nothing other than a tragic human failing. All too human, alas.

In many ways, I think many people have misunderstood or misinterpreted what John Holt had to say about learning, and therefore discounted it. He was fond of saying that children were good at learning, that they don't need to be made to learn or to be shown how, and that what we need to do is give them *access* to the world, to people, places, tools, resources, and so on, and as much help and assistance as they ask for, not more. I think many thought John was implying that, since children were good at learning, therefore they *would* learn everything they needed to know as long as they had access to it. All one had to do was to get rid of the nasty element of coercion, and then children would effortlessly and joyfully learn all the things we want them to know. But I don't think John *was* saying this. He knew that there were no guarantees when it came to learning. He knew that when we try to ensure or guarantee certain outcomes, that's when we get into trouble. In the revised edition of *How Children Learn* (1964/1982), John wrote, "All I am saying in this book can be summed up in two words: Trust Children" (1983, p. xii). If being *good at learning* meant that learning would be automatic or guaranteed, then we wouldn't need to trust children. We only need to have trust and faith in something or someone when we don't know the outcome, when the outcome is not guaranteed, when it might *not* happen.

Similarly, if John Holt were alive today, I think he would be saddened by the efforts of some people who try to turn his term "unschooling" into some sort of a system, into a set of rules that must be followed. John trusted *parents* to learn from their experience with their children. He didn't say, "If you're going to call it *unschooling*, you're going to have to do it my way." He wanted them to figure out what was right for them, for their whole family. His advice and ideas were available as guidance for those who wanted it, but he didn't want to turn unschooling into—of all things—a type of curriculum for parents. This, I feel, was to his credit. It revealed the deep humility of the man.

This humility was also reflected in the way he lived. Despite the financial success of several of his books, John Holt lived rather modestly, as revealed by Mel Allen (1981, December) in the touching portrait of Holt he wrote for *Yankee* magazine.

> John Holt has a shower in his apartment, but he never uses it. When he wants to bathe, he places a green plastic dishpan in his bathtub. He puts a few gallons of

water in it. He gets in the tub and stands in a larger plastic tray designed for catching crankcase oil. He dips a sponge into the water and squeezes it over his body, the water collecting beneath. When he's finished, he carries the water through his kitchen to a small courtyard, where he pours it onto a pile of leaves and garbage. He keeps earthworms in the courtyard and they feed on the pile, making compost.

I absolutely loved this about John. Not only did he see things clearly, but he took action on them. "We have to save water and turn waste into soil," Holt explained. Since he didn't own a car, John walked everywhere or took public transportation. And when he walked, he would always carry a bag with him so that he could pick up trash along the way. "It's my contribution, however small, to a situation I can't do much to change," Holt would say, not without a trace of irritation. Here he was, a famous author, picking up other people's carelessly discarded trash. John Holt practiced what he preached, and any discrepancy between his beliefs and his actions distressed him deeply, until he could get them into greater alignment. I think of him often in this regard and strive to emulate his moral consistency (though not always successfully).

Ivan Illich once described John Holt, affectionately, as "a beautifully monomaniacal guy" (as cited in Cayley, 1992, p. 208). While it's true that John never tired of talking about children and learning, because he felt he had something important to say on those matters, in many ways he was far from monomaniacal. He had many varied interests. He cared deeply about ecology, politics, art, economics, psychology, food and agriculture (he once thought of becoming a farmer), the effects of technology on society, and especially music. He cared deeply about the natural world and, once again, saw so clearly where we are headed. This was revealed so poignantly at the very end of his life, as recorded by his friend George Dennison:

> In the last weeks of his life John spent eight days with us at our home in Maine. Something happened one day that gave me a glimpse of the very heart of his life. He was so weak he could only walk a few steps at a time and with canes. It was beautiful weather. I took him driving to see the views from certain hills—long views of wooded slopes, fields, streams, our large river, and several ponds. Again and again he said, "How beautiful it is!" He was sitting beside me in the front seat. We drove on and he began to talk about his work. "It could

be such a wonderful world," he said, "such a wonderful place." His body began to shake and he dropped his head, crying uncontrollably—but he kept talking through the sobs, his voice strained and thin. "It's not as if we don't know what to do," he said. "We know *exactly* what to do, and it would work, it would work. They're going to wreck it." (as cited in Sheffer, 1990, p. 276)

They, or rather we, *are* wrecking it. In those uncontrollable sobs, John bore witness to the fact that our entire way of life—which includes the way we raise children—is destroying the planet, is using up nature, which he loved so dearly, and replacing it with waste. As I look upon what's happening around me, as I contemplate the fate of the world, if I can stand to look at it with an unflinching eye, John's final pronouncement comes back to haunt me. Our love of comfort and convenience, of power and control, our need to turn the world into a machine to guarantee favorable outcomes (and what is school if not a social machine?), our penchant for replacing genuine care and love with the ministrations of impersonal institutions, our inability or unwillingness to live modestly and accept limits—all this is what is doing the wrecking.

I consider myself very fortunate to have encountered John Holt. Though I only knew him a short while, his influence was profound and enduring. Through his writings and our too few but wonderful conversations, he opened my mind to many important ideas that I carry with me to this day. His writings also introduced me to other important thinkers, most notably to Ivan Illich, with whom I carried on a long and fruitful friendship, and, indirectly, to Susannah Sheffer, with whom I carry on an even longer and different type of relationship. I miss John very much these days and selfishly wish he had lived even a few years longer. At age 89, he could conceivably still be alive today. How I would cherish his perspective, his wisdom, his intellect, his integrity, his humility, his playfulness, his deadpan humor, and above all else, his clarity of vision.

References

Allen, M. (1981, December). The education of John Holt. *Yankee Magazine*. Retrieved from www.holtgws.com/educationofjh.html

Cayley, D. (1992). *Ivan Illich in Conversation.* Concord, On: House of Anansi.

Farenga, P., Ricci, C., & Tedesco, S. (Eds.) (in press). *Growing without schooling.* Medford, MA: HoltGWS LLC.

Graubard, A. (1974). *Free the Children: Radical Reform and the Free School Movement.* Vintage Books, 1972, 1974, p. 267. (Original work published 1972)

Holt, J., & Farenga, P. (2003). *Teach your own: The John Holt book of homeschooling* (Revised ed.). USA: Da Capo Press. (Original work published 1981)

Holt, J. (2004). *Instead of education: Ways to help people do things better.* Boulder, CO: Sentient Publications. (Original work published 1976)

Holt, J. (1984, April). "Why teachers fail." *The Progressive.* Retrieved from www.holtgws.com/writingbyjohnhol.html.

Holt, J. (1983). *How children learn* (Revised ed.). USA: Da Capo Press. (Original work published 1967)

Holt, J. (1982). *How children fail* (Revised ed.). USA: Da Capo Press. (Original work published 1964)

Holt, J. (1974, April 8). "Imagining the future: The learning society . . ." *The Christian Science Monitor.*
Retrieved from
www.holtgws.com/writingbyjohnhol.html

Holt, J., (Producer), & Hughes, P. (Director). (1974). *We have to call it school.* USA: Holt Associates.

The National Commission on Excellence in Education (1983, April). *A nation at risk: The imperative for educational reform.* Retrieved from
datacenter.spps.org/uploads/SOTW_A_Nation_at_Risk_1983.pdf

Sheffer, S. (Ed.). (1990). *A life worth living: Selected letters of John Holt.* USA: Ohio State University Press.

Aaron Falbel considers himself extremely fortunate to have known both John Holt and Ivan Illich personally, as these men have greatly influenced his outlook on learning and society. Aaron's writings have been published in *Growing Without Schooling*, *Peacework*, *Plain*, and *Mothering* magazines, and elsewhere. He is currently an organic farm worker and part-time librarian in Western Massachusetts.

Homeschooling Makes It Easier for Your Life to Be All of a Piece

By Jenny Wright

We discovered *Growing Without Schooling* when it first started: issue number 1! We immediately subscribed—and I wrote a long letter to John and *GWS* and it got published in *GWS* number 8, "Growing with Trees" (1978). I am rereading it now. The first paragraph succinctly sums up what *GWS*, John's newsletter, meant to me. And his long reply in the newsletter shows more of that understanding, encouragement, and support.

Growing With Trees

I read *How Children Learn* when Vanessa was 2 and felt helped by it to see ways of playing and communicating that I'd been missing. I heard part of a lecture you gave on public radio about kids having the right to work and be part of the "real" world. But I didn't know until *GWS* #1 came out that you'd gone all the way to *no school*. At that time Vanessa was 8 and had never gone to school. It was so exciting to hear that there even *were* any others. *GWS* has filled a real need, helping us feel less alone and more faith in what we are doing.

Stan, Vanessa, and I . . . earn almost all of our money by seasonal orchard work—picking apples 2 months in the fall and pruning apple trees 2 months in the late winter. We leave home and work in various parts of (apple country). I've been doing this since I was 4 months pregnant with Vanessa. She is almost 10. The other 8 months we are home, in a neighborhood with 6 or so other couples who also live in the woods, are building their own houses. Most garden, most are self-employed doing crafts or odd jobs. Vanessa's best friend—Melissa (8)—is also her cousin and also has never been to school. She's enrolled in the Santa Fe

Community School. We are "keeping a low profile." Neither of our families have been bothered by the law. Vanessa and Melissa play with other kids in the area who do go to school. We don't hide what we're doing but we don't advertise it either. I don't really know how much the local school board knows and whether or not they're purposely looking the other way. (Ed [John Holt]—this is often the case.) Since we three leave home Sept. 1st and March 1st each time for 2 months, it is possible they just assume she goes to school somewhere else. [. . .]

I don't believe in compelling kids to study some subject they don't want to, but I do believe in insisting they do some work, in relation to their abilities and the needs of the family. Since they start with a compelling desire to do what the older family members do, this is no problem. Now sometimes she objects to some chores ("It's boring, so-and-so doesn't have to."). We insist. If you want to be warm, too, you have to carry firewood, too. She seems to see the justice of it and gives in pretty easily. She helps with pruning, too. Has her own saw and with direction will sometimes prune a whole tree. But it is a harder skill to learn.

I think living on a work crew has been really good for our family. It helped me set limits and encouraged us to accept time away from each other, but still allowed us to be together when we needed it. Very young, Vanessa accepted that I had to work and learned to amuse herself very well. I think that kind of solitude is very important for everyone. She became less clinging and demanding and learned I could choose which demands I would meet. Before crew life I felt I should give her everything she was asking for. As a result of working with her near, I learned that she could accept it and benefitted when I sometimes let her work it out herself. This led to both of us feeling our own individuality and made our close times closer. And brought my way of being with her into accord with Stan's way.

Since I have been the bookkeeper on the last few crews, her interest in math has grown sharply. She helps with the payroll and counts out everyone's final net pay.

She seems to have a good solid concept of reading and math. She doesn't gobble them up in quantity but when she's interested in something she follows it through. Here some of my insecurity about her comes cropping up. How does she compare with other kids her age? I can remember doing more at her age with school stuff (naturally) and being more interested in reading and music and kids' games. But I lived in a city neighborhood, went to school and had 2 sisters, and my parents were more intellectual. All in all, the hardest thing about not sending Vanessa to school is the unknown. Since school was such a big part of my life, I can't imagine what it would have been like without it (especially ages 13–18). It's hard to imagine what her life will be without it. Looking back—so far, so good, but looking ahead is one big question mark. Will she be equipped with what she needs to be independent of us? Will she have friends enough during adolescence? She doesn't ask to go to school; will she try it later? I think we need to do more to help her have access to other parts of the world and help her follow through with more of her interests. Pottery, sewing, cooking, and French are some. These aren't my strong interests or skills and so it will be with friends that she pursues them. We'll continue sending her over to our potter friend's house. We've just found a French woman living not too far away. Maybe she'll tutor Vanessa in French. I'd like for her to try out more extracurricular but school-type things. She was in a swimming class last summer. 4-H? I sometimes feel unsure in how much to encourage or make things happen for her and how much to wait and let her initiate. I wonder if we'll get hassled by the law sometime in the future. (Wright, 1978. pp. 5–6)

[John's] **REPLY**

You wonder how Vanessa compares with other kids her age? My guess would be that she compares very well, probably smarter, more self-reliant, more serious, more considerate, more self-motivated, more independent, more honest, etc.

> I think of the exclusive and expensive school where I first taught fifth grade. My students were the children of many of the leading business, professional, and academic families in this area. I would guess that the average family income must have been at least $40,000 a year [In 1970s dollars—Eds.], and the average IQ of the children over 120. I worked with three fifth grade classes there, sixty children, grew fond of them, came to know them well. But I felt very strongly that of that group of children not one in four, if even that many, had the kind of health of mind and spirit that I would have wanted for a child of my own. And I suspect they were better than their counterparts at that same school today, for these are harder and more anxious times for children to grow up in. You say that as a kid her age you were more interested in reading. I was too. But in the school I just mentioned, I can't remember more than a handful of those super-bright children who ever read for fun. At 10 and 11, I read a great deal, on my own. By the time I was 13, away at boarding school, this had stopped. I had plenty of time at school, since I found the work easy, but I can't remember ever, not even once, reading a book that had not been assigned. Many of those that were assigned, I loved—Joseph Conrad, for instance. But I never read any of his other books, just for my own pleasure. If she needs your help she will ask for it. Meanwhile, if your own life and the lives of other adults around you that she knows are rich and satisfying, that will be the best possible example and encouragement for her. And unlike most children, she will not only have seen but shared most of the best parts of your lives. (Holt, 1978. pp. 6–7)

I continued to subscribe until it sadly and without warning folded. I still have my complete set in a file cabinet, and sometimes refer to it still. Aaron Falbel's pieces, for example.

John came to visit here once with his cello. We live a half-hour away from where the Wallaces lived then and he split a visit between us (his first visit to the Wallaces, I think), after giving a talk in Keene, NH.

He brought his cello and played for us and we went on a hike to some cliffs and a beaver pond.

We also corresponded during and after the time Stan and I had a sick newborn who died at three weeks after some very invasive medical procedures. Unlike most of our friends and relatives, John could understand our distress and ambivalence at the approach taken by the doctors. And he could understand our questioning whether intervention or treatment is always the right thing. Some looked at our questioning as us not loving the baby, or as fanaticism against technology, and so on; John did not do that. And his understanding was important to me. Now, after reading Ivan Illich and knowing of John's friendship with him, I am not surprised.

6/21/82

Dear Jenny,

The morning mail brought your simple and eloquent card about the death of your little baby. I'm so sorry— and it made me all the sorrier that as I read it I could see our little one-year-old visitor Anna, who comes in often when her mother Mary comes in to do volunteer work. I kept looking at this enchanting baby and thinking, "Poor Jenny and Stan will never get to see Nora at one year old, just starting to walk and talk."

Death is always sad, but saddest of all in the case of little children, because we think of all the life they did not have and will not have.

I first encountered this in a personal way when my sister Jane's little boy Christopher, then about a year and a half, escaped his watchers for a crucial minute or two, fell into a swimming pool, and drowned. It almost killed my sister. In time she recovered enough to go on with life— on the whole a busy and happy life—but she never forgot that baby, or (to this day) stopped wondering if he was alive now what he might be like and what he might be doing. I think I can say with confidence that such thoughts no longer cause her actual pain, but she will always be curious about what that little person might have been, and I would guess you will always be curious as well.

I can hardly even begin to guess what it was like to hold your little baby and feel her life slipping slowly away. The only thing I could offer in the way of possibly useful advice about a way to deal with the pain of that memory is paradoxical—instead of trying to forget it, try to remember it. The memory will remain, but a distance may develop between you and the memory; instead of it being like reliving the event, it will be more like watching a film of the event, and then perhaps in time a photo of it, then a black and white photo, then a drawing, a sketch.

It must be infuriating to think, "If those high-powered dummies had only had enough sense to figure out what was wrong with the poor little critter, they might have been able to fix it!" I guess such thoughts will be with you a long time. Again, I would not try to prevent myself from thinking them.

But I'm so sorry, and so sad, for you, and partly because I had been looking forward to seeing and making friends with your little baby.

love,

John

(J. Holt, personal communication, June 21, 1982)

7/1/82

Dear Jenny,

A beautiful day today, nicest we've had since I got back from Europe. A big Polar High has moved in from the North, air is clear and fresh, not a cloud in the sky, lovely cool breeze blowing, hot bright sun—perfect! And you may think, all those days that little Nora will never see. Never see snow. All those things! A sad thought. But I think it will be better not to push that thought away from you, but when it comes, think it fully. Maybe even, when a nice day, or snow, or some other miracle comes along, look at it twice, once for you and once for Nora, enjoy it a little more than you would, as if you could send her a share of your pleasure.

Easier for me to say than for you to do, I know. But I think you can do it and I think it will help. It's terrible about those doctors, and I agree with you 100%! Of course there are some good ones, and I even know a couple. But by and large I distrust and fear them. Some things they know how to do—fix broken bones, sew up big cuts. A few diseases they really do know how to treat and cure, though as Illich said (do you know his *Medical Nemesis*?) those diseases could easily be diagnosed and treated by a person with six months training, we don't need $100,000-a-year doctors to deal with them.

In one sense it is certain that doctors mean well; that is, they much prefer their patients to recover than to die. In other senses I don't think they mean well at all. A great many of them went into medicine mostly for the money, which they admit frankly. They think of themselves partly as highly skilled repairmen (repairpersons? ugh!), fixing complicated machines which just happen to be alive. They are very clever problem solvers, and see their patients as problems, or perhaps as the carriers of problems which they have to solve. In a more heroic sense they see themselves as fighters in a never-ending war against two entities called Disease and Death. They fight these enemies with the weapons of Science and Technology, with fancy machines. And they see their patients as a kind of battlefield on which this war is fought, as the Pentagon saw Vietnam as a battlefield on which we waged our endless war against Communism. What counted was to win the war, not Vietnam. In the same way, what counts for doctors is to win a victory over Disease and Death—which means to postpone Death—no matter what the cost of this victory may be to the patient. They have an ideology about this which allows them to do anything in that war. They say, "If we learn how to defeat Disease and Death, then future generations of people will be spared all that suffering." So any suffering they may cause in the here-and-now seems to them a worthy, not to say holy, cause. In this cause there is practically no limit to the amount of suffering they are willing to inflict on the here-and-now patient, just as the torturers of the Inquisition, believing they were saving souls from eternal damnation and hell fire, were willing to cause limitless pain in order to get heretics to confess, and so save their souls. I admit the comparison is in some ways unfair—but not too much so. Those doctors were fighting against Death, not for your little baby.

As you rightly say, if they had known what the trouble was with Nora, and had had any reasonable expectation that all their torments might cure it, there could have been something said for it. What bugs me about them is that when they don't know what to do, they experiment—let's try this, who knows, it might work. This is a violation of their own Hippocratic oath, which says, "Do no harm." It is scientifically bad and ethically and morally outrageous. They say, in effect, "We don't know how to cure you, but if we do enough things to you we may be able to learn something that might cure you, or even if it doesn't, might someday cure someone else." Even this might be defensible if they said to the patient, "Listen, we don't know what's wrong with you or we don't know what to do about it, but we have some ideas about experiments that we might do from which we might learn something, is it OK with you if we do them?" I see no reason why the patients should pay for these experiments; on the contrary, if doctors want to use us as laboratory animals, it seems more reasonable that they should pay us. And they should be honest with us about what the experiments will cost us in discomfort, pain, etc. and what the realistic chances are of their learning something. But they never do this, they never come clean about what they know and don't know, they act as if they know everything, and there are very few of them who don't get furiously indignant if their patients ask them questions about their treatments.

Have you read Norman Cousins' *Anatomy of an Illness* (on our list)? He saved himself because he began to realize that the doctors didn't know what was wrong with him, and that if he was going to get well he was going to have to find out himself what was wrong with him and how it might be treated. One of the terrible realities you will have to live with, as you are living with it, is that you will never know whether it was disease, or medicine, that killed Nora. I don't think you can help yourself from asking the question, but I think it is futile to guess the answer—it just has to be one of those permanently unanswered questions we all have to live with.

For myself, I make it my business to stay out of the hands of the doctors if I possibly can—and I have been able to. It scares me to think that when I get old I may not be able to keep myself out of their hands. I have a vision of myself getting very old, and realizing that soon I will be too old and weak to take care of myself, and then going out for a long walk in the woods to die, like an old Eskimo. But maybe that is just a (fairly) young man's fantasy, and vanity, and ignorance. In the end, we cling pretty hard to life.

A story. Something like eight years or so ago I had a little black growth removed from the calf of my left leg. I had noticed it there for some time, and had thought about removing it. One day a friend of mine saw it, asked about it, and with one thing and another made an appointment for me with a dermatologist to get the thing taken off. I showed up in his office, he snipped it off, put in a stitch or two, slapped on a bandage, and I left. Fine. Later the plot thickened. The doctor called me up, said he had sent the little growth to a lab, that two of the doctors who had seen it had said it was benign but the third was not quite sure, and that the doctor had made an appointment for me to see a cosmetic (plastic) surgeon so that he could (as they say) take some more tissue off—just to be sure. On the day I went to this other surgeon's office, after a long delay, I was ushered into a dressing room and pulled up my trouser leg to expose scar. Another long wait. Finally, in came a very brisk young doctor and a nurse. Doctor looked at scar a second or two, then said, "Can you make an appointment with Dr. Anastasi (something like that) at his hospital in Danvers on Sept. XX? What we plan to do is remove a piece of tissue about the size of an old silver dollar, going down to the fascia (muscle sheath). Then we will have to do a plastic surgery graft, using skin from your thigh. You should be in hospital about eight or nine days." In a bit of a daze I said I thought I could be there, and would confirm the date. Then the doc and nurse moved briskly on to the next examining room, leaving me to pull my pants leg down and get out of the office on my own. I went off, feeling swept away by powerful forces. Not until I got in the cab did I begin to think, "Now wait a minute, let's take a look at this. Here's this surgeon, Anastasi, all set to do an operation and skin graft on a man he will never have seen until he operates on him. What kind of medicine is this? Suppose someone gets the tag wrong, and the tag says that the leg is to come off—how will the doc know the difference?" The more I thought about that way of doing medicine, the less I liked it. I seemed to be setting myself up for medical malpractice. Suppose the graft didn't take? Suppose there were complications, and then someone said, "Just to be sure the carcinoma hasn't got into the lymph glands, maybe we'd better remove a few of them—just to be sure?" Where might it end?

The upshot of it all was that, riding along in the cab, I made a decision. As soon as I got home I called the surgeon's office and cancelled the appointment. Later I told the dermatologist that I had done so, and asked him to send the slides of my little black spot to another hospital for confirmation. I never heard from them. In doing all this I made a decision, which I had talked about with Illich on a theoretical basis but now had to put into action. I might die of cancer if I had to, but I was sure as hell not going to die of medicine. It was a very liberating feeling.

I am sufficiently persuaded by Linus Pauling's statistics about the effectiveness of large doses of Vitamin C in halting the spread of cancer so that I am taking 5 grams a day, just as a kind of insurance. If I should develop what looks like a more serious cancer I will probably increase the dose, and also do something about diet. Maybe get some laetrile. What I will do for sure is run as fast as I can go in the opposite direction from Mass. General Hospital. I doubt very much whether I would go to a hospital even for a fairly serious heart attack. A friend of mine is in MGH right now for some big bypass valve job.

I hope it works out, and it probably will—this seems to be one of those things they know how to do. But I would have done it with diet, rest, exercise.

About the rights of parents to decide about treatment for their children. Like many other things, this varies somewhat from state to state and even from judge to judge. You remember the case of Chad Green here in Mass. He was 4 or 5, very sick with leukemia. The parents wanted to treat him with vitamins and diet, the doctors wanted the high-tech medicine number. A judge ruled that the Green's had to follow the wishes of the doctors. They left the state, and as it turned out the little boy died about a year later. But in an almost identical case a judge in New York State ruled in favor of the family, saying that there was little or no evidence that this kind of medical intervention did in fact increase life expectancy. So some judges will rule one way, others another. In general, I would guess that most of them would come down on the side of the doctors. We are much in the grip of expert worship.

Glad Vanessa was able to handle the situation, and glad that she is getting along OK.

Things going along here. Slight slump in subs and book business, partly because the post office is refusing to forward mail sent to 308, which is about 1/3 to 1/2 of our total mail. Could be a bit of a serious problem, if we can't straighten it out.

Did I tell you I bought a new cello, brand new, at a famous school in Germany. Much better than anything I have used. Such a relief not to have to fight the instrument.

I told Elizabeth [Gravelos] and Arthur [Harvey] that I would spend a day or so with the picking crew in the fall. But my lecture schedule for those months is getting more and more crowded, so I might have to take a rain check, though I really would like to go, and will if I can.

Once again, I'm so sorry that your little baby died, and about the way of her dying. I think you did all you could. Live one day at a time, do what must be done, and try now and then to look at the world as if you were looking *for* Nora. Write again whenever you feel like, and no editing, please!

love to all,
John

(J. Holt, personal communication, July 1, 1982)

July—Yesterday cloudy, but another heavenly day today. Huge crowds gathered at the edge of the river to hear the music and watch the fireworks, which I will watch myself—I love them, yell out loud like a kid. They are so beautiful, and the big bangs are nice, though I might not like them so much if I had heard bombs go off.

Am writing to add a second word on the medical story. Had lunch with an old friend today, the one whose husband had the heart operation. When they took the old valve out of his heart, it was so hardened it was like bone. That particular valve works like the iris in the eye or the aperture of a camera, and it had become so hard that there was just a teeny little hole that the heart had to squeeze the blood through. The doctors say that if they hadn't found it and done their operation, which seems to have gone just fine, he would probably have died suddenly during the year. Of course, they might be wrong. If they are right, they saved his life. How can I argue with that?

The replacement valve came from a pig, raised in Taiwan in super-hygienic environments and killed at just the instant when its heart was most like the size and shape of a human heart. So there is modern medicine at its best. This same friend's first husband has within the last year or so had an operation for a brain tumor that would almost certainly have killed him if it hadn't been removed. He was already losing his balance and beginning to lose his sight when they took it out. He is much better now, though not fully recovered.

Suppose I suddenly began to have violent headaches, and lost the sight of an eye, and couldn't stand up straight, and suppose they said, "You have a brain tumor." Would I take that walk in the woods that I talked about? Or would I go to the hospital? If I thought the operation would leave me a vegetable, I'd say the hell with it. But if I thought there was a pretty good chance I'd get my health back and stay in action for a while longer, I'd probably do that. Not an easy question.

And yet, and yet, in many ways I stick to what I said, that in many ways I don't trust modern medicine.

(J. Holt, personal communication, July 4, 1982.)

I visited John to say goodbye when his cancer was very advanced. He was staying with the Van Dorens and I was eight and a half months pregnant. I brought him some ripe peaches from our trees, but he could hardly eat. He tried, though. The only thing I can remember him talking about that day was childbirth and how women knowingly face and accept the pain of it.

Our son Willis was born on the day of John's memorial service so, of course, I missed it.

So that's about it. I felt shy and nervous with him in person—my insecurity with people I respect a lot and don't know very well. We were in each other's presence only four or five times. But in letter writing, having more time to collect my thoughts, I felt very connected.

Our family homeschooled—unschooled, really—the whole way (through high school). For the most part, I'm glad. It's impossible to know what another path would have led to.

Vanessa (43) and Willis (26) are both doing fine. David (26) is struggling, but would he have been struggling anyway?

When I start talking about our family, I get lost in generalities or swamped in details. And you're not asking about us, really. John Holt and GWS were a big influence and unschooling was a big part of our family life. So was living without running water or electricity, reading aloud for hours night after night, building our own house, spending a lot of time outdoors, working and living communally on apple picking and pruning crews. John Holt's influence was one part of this life that all went together, was "all of a piece."

Homeschooling makes it easier for your life to be all of a piece—not only in the way we did it, but in many different ways and places.

References

Cousins, N. (1979) *Anatomy of an illness as perceived by the patient.* New York, NY: W.W.W. Norton & Company, Inc.

Farenga, P., Ricci, C., & Tedesco, S. (Eds.) (in press). *Growing without schooling.* Medford, MA: HoltGWS LLC.

Holt, J. (1978). Reply. *Growing without schooling, 8,* 6–7.

Holt, J. (1983). *How children learn* (Revised ed.). USA: Da Capo Press. (Original work published 1967).

Illich, I. (2002). *Limits to medicine: Medical Nemesis: The expropriation of health.* New York, NY: Marion Boyars Publishers LTD. (Original work published 1976).

Wright, J. (1978). Growing with trees. *Growing without schooling, 8,* 5–6.

Jenny Wright: From a very young age I was interested in subsistence living, traditional crafts, and nature study. I found a home in New Hampshire with seasonal orchard workers and homesteaders. The crews were full of idealists, exposing each other to radical ideas—voluntary poverty, non-violent activism, raw food diets, different religions, artists, craftspeople, and musicians.

Stan and I met in this setting and raised our family, partly on the crews and partly in the back-to-the-land neighborhood that became Quaker City Land Trust. We're still here forty years later, still teaching and leading crews for picking and pruning, still adding new interests and skills: Stan is section-hiking the Appalachian Trail and I am getting better at beekeeping and spoon-carving.

www.ingramcontent.com/pod-product-compliance
Lightning Source LLC
Chambersburg PA
CBHW052036070526
44584CB00016B/2069